Reading through Hebrews

Reading through Hebrews

C.R.Hume

SCM PRESS LTD

0 334 02689 X

First published 1997 by
SCM Press Ltd
9–17 St Albans Place London N I ONX

Typeset at The Spartan Press Ltd,
Lymington, Hants
Printed in Great Britain by
Biddles Ltd,
Guildford and King's Lynn

Contents

Foreword

This book has been written with the aim of encouraging ordinary Christians to study the Bible in a straightforward and sustained way. Some years ago I began running short courses on passages from the letters of the New Testament for fellow Christians in Monmouth. These courses became an annual feature and in 1994–5 a course on the whole of the letter to the Hebrews was held over eight evenings. Friends suggested publication, so here is a guide based on my lecture notes. How should it be used?

Although this book may be read by an individual, it can be used when a group is studying the letter together. The leader of the group may consult it when preparing a passage for general discussion or it can be used by individual members where resources allow the purchase of more than one copy. Better still, if it can be used in an ecumenical setting where people from different churches can together explore the scriptures that we all share. It could also be used by an 'A' level class of students. Incidentally, it is an advantage if the group brings different translations of the letter to the study sessions. That can certainly provoke some interesting discussion!

I believe that we need nowadays to return to a more disciplined reading of the Bible. My aim has been to concentrate on the actual meaning of the text in the context of the first century. So this guide attempts primarily to face the question 'What did this mean when it was written?' Ordinary Christians are put off using commentaries because they often discuss at length academic or theological questions but leave the basic text unexplained. Such commentaries have their place, but for anyone who wants to read, perhaps for the first time, a letter from the New Testament, the simpler (and the shorter!) the guide, the better it is for the reader.

No Greek words referred to in this book are printed in Greek characters. People are interested in the meaning of the Greek terms, so they appear here in a form that those who know no Greek can easily read.

The letter to the Hebrews is not immediately accessible to the average reader, who can be put off by the rabbinical tone of the letter which piles quotation upon quotation. It is, however, worth the effort, for behind the academic veneer there is a strong emotion and a burning faith which flashes out in some of the most sublime passages to be found in the New Testament.

Introduction

Authorship and date

From earliest times the authorship of the Epistle to the Hebrews has been in dispute. The fact, however, that the church later came to the belief that the author was St Paul tells us that the document was regarded as important and of the same rank as those letters known to be the product of Paul's hand. Why is there a problem in ascribing the letter to St Paul? The style, vocabulary and grammar of the work all show many differences when compared with anything generally accepted as Pauline. Yet the theology fits so well that of Paul, despite the attempts of some modern commentators to over-emphasize apparent differences, that we should be looking for an author who was either a contemporary and possibly close friend of Paul or one who was very familiar with Paul's works. Calvin, who concluded that Paul was not the author, felt that the authorship of the letter was not important and that it should be accepted without controversy as an apostolic epistle.

There are some clues which might help to narrow the field. Firstly, the fact that the author seems to assume throughout the letter that the Temple in Jerusalem was still in operation points to a date before AD 70 (the year of the fall of Jerusalem and the destruction of the Temple by the Romans). Secondly, there are strong indications that the author was influenced in his approach to the scriptures by such writers as Philo of

Alexandria, a Jewish writer of the first century AD, whose commentaries on scripture are characterized by the use of allegory and whose theology was heavily influenced by the Hellenistic philosophy of neo-Platonism, which portrayed this material world as an inferior copy of an eternal one, and thus heaven was seen as the spiritual goal of the immortal human soul struggling to escape from the prison of the flesh. The influence of Philo should not be over-emphasized; for example, there is no indication in the letter to the Hebrews that the author saw matter as impeding the immortal soul's progress. For our writer matter is not the enemy nor does he describe the soul as intrinsically immortal. The differences between Philo and our writer are discussed in more detail by Montefiore.[1] In this connection it should be mentioned that all the references in the letter to the Hebrews to the Old Testament seem to derive from the Septuagint, the Greek translation of the Bible created by the Alexandrian Jewish scholars. Thirdly, the work seems to have been known by Clement of Rome, who quotes from this letter around 95.

Lastly, familiarity with Temple ritual may point to an author who was one of the priestly caste, a member of the tribe of Levi, while his excellent Greek indicates an education in a Gentile Hellenistic community. What did the earliest scholars say?

Tertullian, whose life straddles the second and third centuries, states[2] that the author was Barnabas. He certainly would fit the requirements. Described in Acts 4.36 as a Levite from Cyprus, he was intimate with Paul from the earliest days, and after being commissioned by the church in Jerusalem as an apostle, worked with Paul in Antioch, Cyprus and many parts of Asia Minor.

---

[1] H. W. Montefiore, *The Epistle to the Hebrews*, A & C Black 1964, 6–8.
[2] *On Chastity*, 20.

Origen, some time after 245, according to Eusebius,[3] says 'Who wrote the Epistle to the Hebrews, only God knows the truth'.

The final piece of evidence pointing to Barnabas is provided by the sixth century Codex Claromontanus, which mentions in a list of all the books of the Bible a letter of Barnabas having 850 lines. As I Corinthians is put down as 1060 lines we can compare the length of the two works and show that this letter of Barnabas is clearly around the same length as our Epistle to the Hebrews. Incidentally, there is extant a spurious letter of Barnabas which seems to have been composed at a later date than the lifetime of our Barnabas, and is very different in style and subject.

Some commentators like to make a connection between the Hebrew meaning of the name Barnabas – 'son of consolation'– and the consolation referred to in Hebrews 13.22, 'I beseech you, brothers and sisters, to put up with my message of **paraklêsis** (i.e. admonishment in this context rather than consolation), for indeed my letter to you is a brief one.' Readers can judge for themselves whether this is evidence for Barnabas' authorship.

Another candidate, put forward by Luther and others, but with little corroborating evidence, is Apollos. More recently such scholars as Harnack have suggested that the work was written by Priscilla. Needless to say, there is no evidence for this candidate either. All we need to know is that the author is a writer of power and skill and one who preaches the essential gospel of Christ.

To whom is the letter addressed?

Unlike other letters in the New Testament, we have no opening formula which should name the recipients, where they lived, and who was writing. Compare the start of the letter to the

---

[3] *The History of the Church*, VI. 25.

Romans, 'Paul, a servant of Jesus Christ . . . to all that are in Rome . . . grace and peace. . . etc.', or the start of Galatians, 'Paul, an apostle . . . and all the brethren which are with me, to the churches of Galatia, grace be to you and peace . . . etc.'

Some have concluded that the work is more of a general treatise, something to be read by a wider audience and not addressed to a particular congregation, in fact, not a letter at all. The end of the work, however, shows quite clearly that this is a letter, because we have the usual little messages one can read in other NT letters, 'Know that our brother Timothy has left and I shall see you with him, if he arrives soon. Greet all your leaders and all the saints. Those from Italy greet you. Grace be with you all.'

What might have happened is that the first few lines were lost. This was not unusual. It was easy, perhaps through over-handling or re-reading, either to break off completely a piece of the papyrus or to damage the surface so badly that the words could no longer be read. It would not be difficult to reconstruct. For example, we could suggest, 'Barnabas, an apostle of Jesus Christ by the will of God, to the saints of the churches of the Hebrews in Rome, grace and peace be to you all.'

Why Rome? And why plural churches? Well, look at the phrase in 13.24, 'Those from Italy greet you.' In Acts 21.27 we have a similar formula, 'the Jews from Asia', which refers to the Jews in Jerusalem who came from Asia Minor. In this context, 'those from Italy' must mean 'those friends of yours who are here with me now', i.e. not *in* Italy, because they are away from home. So, if we are looking for a likely place in Italy for the recipients of the letter to be living, we are driven to the conclusion that it must be Rome. Where else in Italy would there be enough Jewish Christians to make such a letter necessary or suitable? If we also assume that there was more than one church, it might go some way to explaining how the letter presumably was damaged, i.e. by being passed around and read out to different congregations. It is, of course, possible that the churches were in Rome and other large conurbations in Italy, such as Naples. Incidentally, the title 'To the Hebrews' is probably not an original part of the text, but rather one attached to the document once it began to circulate in the church. Several manuscripts, after saying 'it was written to the Hebrews', add intriguing phrases such as, 'from Rome', or 'from Italy', and 'through (or by the means of) Timothy', or 'from Paul the apostle to those in Jerusalem', or even 'in Hebrew from Italy anonymously through Timothy'. We need not expect too much from such obvious guesses.

But all this is mere guesswork. Here is another problem.

Why 'Hebrews' and not 'Jews', **Hebraioi** and not **Ioudaioi**? One reason is that already the term 'Jew' is coming to mean 'non-Christian'. In other words, 'Jews' = 'those who follow the law of the Old Testament'. So the word 'Hebrews' will be used to refer to Christian Jews, i.e. those who have accepted Jesus as Messiah and Saviour. Could it mean 'those speaking Hebrew or Aramaic'? In the Gentile world, and especially in the western part of the Roman Empire, it is quite likely that the normal language of the Jews would tend to be Greek. This is not to say that they could not understand Hebrew as a scholarly language or not speak Aramaic, as many of their relations living in Palestine or Syria would have done in daily life. But the fact that this letter is written in Greek, and that the texts of the Old Testament quoted throughout are taken from the Greek Septuagint, is strong evidence for saying that the term 'Hebrews' in this context has a cultural and ethnic application rather than a linguistic one.

The reference in one of the manuscripts referred to above which states that Hebrew was the original language in which the letter was composed is interesting. Could it be that scholars, aware of the differences between this letter and others known to be by Paul, accounted for them by putting forward the hypothesis that these differences were due to the fact that the letter had been translated into Greek and was not, unlike his other letters, originally composed in that language? What is even more interesting is the statement that the recipients lived in Jerusalem. Is this possible?

Firstly, the letter was originally composed in Greek. There is no way we can treat the text as a translation from Hebrew (or Aramaic). It has none of the feel of a translation. The phrasing, the metaphors, indeed, the rhythm and style are Greek, and the quotations from the O T are from the Septuagint, not translated from the original Hebrew. Secondly, the church in Jerusalem was composed of Gentiles as well as Jewish Christians. The intended audience for our letter seems to be entirely Jewish, so far as we can judge from the arguments used throughout by the author, and from the very first sentence which refers to God speaking 'to *our* fathers by the prophets'. It is hard to imagine a Gentile audience being addressed in this way.

In conclusion, it appears that the title 'to the Hebrews' may have suggested to later readers that the recipients lived in Judaea. But we know from several sources that the term 'Hebrew' refers to all Jews, whether in Palestine or the Diaspora, and we can look to many cities, such as Rome, Corinth or Alexandria, as possible candidates. Rome remains the most likely, because of the reference in 13.24 to the greetings of those from Italy.

The use of texts and methods of argument

It is very easy for a modern reader to misunderstand the way our writer deals with his subject. This applies, firstly, in the use of scriptural references, where we tend to take the simple view that the text has one meaning. In other words, as far as we are concerned, the text is either an account of an actual event or a symbolic representation of some theological insight. For example, the story of Noah's ark might be regarded by some as a factual account, by others as an allegory of the church, i.e. Christ building a vehicle to save the believer from death. For our writer, and indeed for most ancient commentators, this was not an issue. Both interpretations are valid. The latter is a deeper interpretation of the former. So when we try to follow the writer's subtle interpretation of the Genesis story relating to Melchizedek, we should avoid falling into the trap of thinking that our writer believed that Melchizedek was only a type of Christ and not a real person, or that in some way Melchizedek actually was Christ. This either/or way of thinking will prevent us from appreciating the riches of our writer's approach. To put it another way, our response to the argument should be emotional as well as rational. We should say, 'Of course, I hadn't thought of that. How marvellous! This is true and that is true as well.' It is not that we are expected to suspend our critical faculty but rather that we should open up our minds and hearts in response to the text, and allow the writer to display the relevance of the text in as many ways as he can. Sometimes there is a philological insight, sometimes a connecting of apparently disparate concepts, sometimes a legalistic line of argument, and sometimes a visionary leap into sublime poetry. A sacred text which has been read and studied so often that it becomes part of the furniture of one's mind is a fertile source of every kind of divine statement.

At this point we should consider the use of allegory by early commentators. There is a tendency for us to think that if a writer uses allegory it must be because he does not believe the passage he is commenting on is a factual account. In other words, we might consider that the fact that Augustine, for example, develops an elaborate interpretation of the Creation story in Genesis on allegorical lines,[4] means that he regarded

---

[4] *Confessions*, Book XIII, *passim*.

the story as a myth. Our modern attitude can be illustrated by considering Bunyan's *Pilgrim's Progress,* where Mr Standfast represents an abstract virtue, and Doubting Castle stands for a psychological state. For us, just because it *is* an allegory, the characters cannot exist in an objective sense – allegory is fiction. It is true that some early Christian writers attacked pagan writers who used allegory to explain away embarrassing accounts of the gods, but the use of allegory by Christian commentators on the scriptures was widespread. An early example of enthusiastic allegorizing is the interpretation of the parable of the Good Samaritan by Origen early in the third century based on an original allegory probably of Irenaeus.[5] The man who fell among thieves represents Adam, Jerusalem is Paradise, Jericho is the world, the bandits are hostile powers, the Samaritan is Christ, the wounds are disobedience, the ass is Christ's body, the inn is the Church, and the Samaritan's promise to return refers to the second coming! Presumably the innkeeper is the Holy Spirit.

It is clear when we consider the use of allegory by Christian and Jewish authors such as Philo that although it is often used to explain a passage whose literal meaning is unacceptable, e.g. references to God having a face, it is just as likely that allegory is being used to draw out some inner meaning from an account whose literal meaning is perfectly acceptable.

Philo used allegory profusely because it was an ideal method for expounding Platonism. The Theory of Ideas, which is the core belief of Platonism, treats material objects as copies of ultimate realities. They are inferior because they are not eternal and because they are imperfect. For the Platonist this world

---

[5] *Homily on Luke* 34, quoted by R. P. C. Hanson, 'Biblical Exegesis in the Early Church', *Cambridge History of the Bible*, Vol. 1, CUP 1970, 418.

furnishes inferior copies of perfect forms which we cannot apprehend with our material senses. Allegory enables Philo to explain the hidden connections between this world of the senses and the other invisible world. The use of allegory, however, is not confined to Platonists. It can be used to bring out hidden meanings in a passage without making any statement about the existential status of the material objects referred to in the passage. In Hebrews we can see both allegory and Platonism, the latter being exemplified in 8.2, which refers to the 'authentic tabernacle', i.e. the perfect and eternal Form of which the earthly shrine is merely a copy. But the fact that our writer has been clearly influenced by Platonism does not mean that he subscribes to its philosophy wholesale, nor does his use of allegory allow such a conclusion.

The central theme

The writer addresses Jewish Christians and consequently bases his arguments on OT texts, particularly the Psalms. He assumes that his audience is familiar with the texts he quotes. There is no hint of any appeal to a non-Jewish audience. Briefly the theme goes as follows:

> 'Scripture shows that Jesus Christ is the son of God, superior not only to all the angels but to Moses and Abraham alike. He has fulfilled the promises of God completely and brought into operation the new covenant which supersedes the old dispensation of the Law. This new covenant has cleansed all from sin more effectively than the former rituals. Do not go back to your old faith but stand firm, despite the temptations and sufferings that threaten you.'

The following plan may help the reader to follow the argument in more detail.

1. *The status of Christ in relation to the angels*

(1.1–3) Up to now God has spoken to us through the prophets but now he has spoken to us by his son. His son was the means through which God created everything and he shares his nature and power. He has effected a perfect atonement of all sin and is now seated at the side of God.

(1.4–14) Christ is greater than the angels because 1. he is the son of God, 2. he created the world and stays unchanged for ever, 3. he sits at God's right hand and shares his power.

(2.1–3) Because Christ is the son of God and superior to angels we must obey his new commandments even more strictly than the old commandments which, although they were mediated to us only by angels, still had to be obeyed.

(2.4–9) The gospel of Christ is supported by the testimony of God, who did not hand over to angels the work of the new creation. Christ's incarnation and death on our behalf have culminated in his glorification.

(2.10–18) Since Christ was responsible for creation it was right for him to lead us into his new creation. His incarnation into our flesh, his suffering and his triumph over death enable us to follow him into glory. It also makes us his brothers. Note that he did not become an angel but a man.

2. *The relation of Christ to Moses*

(3.1–6a) Jesus was faithful like Moses, but Moses was only one of the household of Israel and not the creator of the household. As creator and son of God, therefore, Jesus is superior in honour to Moses.

3. *The need for us to remain faithful*

(3.6b-19) We are part of this household if we remain faithful and do not follow the example of the disobedient Israelites in the wilderness. They did not attain the promised rest of God.

(4.1–11) We still have a chance to attain the eternal Sabbath rest of God, provided we remain faithful.

(4.12–16) We cannot fool God – he sees into our very marrow – but we can find mercy since we have an effective mediator in Christ the high priest who shares our sufferings.

4. *Christ the high priest – an introduction*

(5.1–10) A high priest, as Aaron was, is appointed by God to offer sacrifices for sin on behalf of his fellow men as well as for his own sins. He is able to empathize with them because he shares their human frailties. Christ, too, was appointed by God as a high priest according to the order of Melchizedek and has become the source of everlasting salvation to all believers.

(5.11–6.3) This is a difficult subject and you are slow learners. You must progress beyond the elementary gospel to a more mature understanding of the faith.

5. *A warning against apostasy*

(6.4–12) It is impossible for a baptized member of the church to repent again after apostasizing. But I am sure you are remaining faithful – I trust you will continue to be so.

(6.13–20) God has made a solemn promise to us and we should cling to the hope he has given us. Jesus, the high priest according to the order of Melchizedek, has gone ahead of us.

6. *Christ the high priest – the main argument*

(7.1–10.18) Christ/Melchizedek is superior to Abraham. The differences between the old order of priests and the new high priest Christ and between the old covenant of Moses and the new covenant. The effectiveness of Christ's sacrifice compared with the old sacrifices of the Mosaic law. (See the notes for a more detailed exposition.)

7. *Our response to the sacrifice of Christ*

(10.19–31) Let us approach with confidence the sanctuary, knowing that we have been purified by Christ's sacrifice. Watch over one another and give encouragement. The punishment that awaits the apostate is fearful.

(10.32–39) Remember how faithfully you behaved during times of persecution in the past. Be patient.

8. *Faith*

(11.1–40) Famous examples of faithfulness.

9. *Final exhortation*

(12.1–11) With such examples before us we should take heart and concentrate on completing the course that lies before us. Look at Jesus and think about his triumph over opposition. Accept the discipline of suffering which God our father gives us.

(12.12–17) Pull yourselves together, keep the peace and be holy. Watch out for anybody letting the side down.

(12.18–29) You have come not to Sinai, the place of terror and gloom, but to the heavenly Jerusalem with its celebrating angels and the souls of the righteous. You are in the presence of God and his son. Obey his commands.

10. *Pastoral charge*

(13.1–7) Love one another, be hospitable, look after those in prison, avoid fornication and adultery. Avoid love of money. Remember your leaders and imitate their faith.

(13.8–15) Do not follow ineffectual dietary laws. We have a more effective source of grace in the sacrifice of Jesus. He suffered outside the city, so we should not hesitate to go out to join him. Our home city is in heaven.

(13.16–19) Do charitable work and share your goods with

others. Obey your leaders. Pray for us, and especially pray that we may meet soon.
(13.20–21) My prayer for you.

11. *Final words and signing off*
(13.22–25) Please put up with my sermon – it is only a short one. Timothy is on his way. Regards to everyone there from all of us here.

The simplicity of the central theme contrasts sharply with the complex pattern by which this theme is developed. It is useful to contrast this letter with Paul's letter to the Galatians. The Galatians are basically Gentiles attracted to some of the practices of the Jewish faith. Paul uses arguments derived from the OT, particularly in reference to Abraham and God's promises to him, but in the main he relies on a direct appeal to their hearts and minds, rather than a series of quotations. The letter to the Hebrews, however, is packed with key texts such as a rabbi might use when arguing some abstruse point of law. The intricate flow of the argument is what makes this letter so fascinating, and we must follow it with attention, if we are to appreciate fully the brilliance of the writer.

Before you start – a few things to note

1. The translation of the Greek is my own, and I have attempted to keep close to the original. This makes the translation rather literal, but at the same time it is easier to pick out individual words or phrases. If the end result is a translation that seems to echo the AV or the RSV, so be it.

2. Certain abbreviations are used throughout. They are as follows:

AV	Authorized Version
NEB	New English Bible
NT	New Testament
OT	Old Testament
RSV	Revised Standard Version
Sept.	Septuagint
Vulg.	Vulgate (the Latin version of the Bible by St Jerome)

3. The commentary will follow the text, which will be given in small extracts. This should make it easier to use when studying individual passages on their own or when time is limited.

4. It would be impossible to acknowledge the contributions of all the scholars, ancient and modern, whose works have assisted the writer of this guide. Two in particular should be mentioned; Chrysostom, whose *Homilies on the Epistle to the Hebrews* have been quoted throughout, mostly in the version originally translated by T. Keble and revised by F. Gardiner in the last century, and H. W. Montefiore, whose *Commentary on the Epistle to the Hebrews* has been the most consulted, if not always followed, of all modern works. The latter's comments on the links between our writer and Alexandrian Platonist Judaism are generally relevant and illuminating. A fuller bibliography is given at the end of the book. Where a commentator is mentioned in the text, the reference will be found in the corresponding part of their work. To help the reader to keep track of the ancient writers I refer to, I append here some abbreviated biographies.

Biographies

Augustine (354–430) Bishop of Hippo in north Africa, who was converted to Christianity from Manichaeism and whose most famous works are his *Confessions* and *The City of God*.

John Chrysostom, 'Golden-mouth' (around 349–407) Bishop of Constantinople famous for his preaching, who died in exile after offending the empress Eudoxia.

Clement of Rome (died around 100) Third or fourth bishop of Rome and reputedly a disciple of Paul and Peter. Wrote two letters to the Corinthians.

Gregory of Nazianzus, 'Theologian' (around 329–89) Bishop first of Sasima then of Constantinople. Collaborated with St Basil on an anthology of the works of Origen.

Ignatius, 'Godbearer' (died around 108) Third bishop of Antioch who was sent to Rome to be martyred. On his journey wrote seven letters to various churches.

Irenaeus (died around 202) Born in Asia. Bishop of Lyons. Like Ignatius, an opponent of Gnosticism. Also martyred.

Jerome (around 345–420) Studied in Rome and spent some time in Constantinople with Gregory. Settled in Bethlehem where he founded four monastic communities. Attacked Pelagianism. Famous for his translation of the Bible into Latin.

Josephus (born around 37) Pharisee who took part in the Jewish rebellion against the Romans. Captured in 67 he settled in Rome. Wrote *The Jewish War* and *Antiquities*. Although pro-Roman he defended the Jewish race and religion against the Alexandrian scholar Apion.

Origen (around 185–254) Christian Platonist and biblical scholar. Taught first in Alexandria and then Palestine where he was ordained priest. Imprisoned and tortured during Decian persecutions.

Philo (around 30 BC–AD 45) Head of Jewish community in Alexandria. Sent as delegate to Rome to ask emperor Caligula for exemption from duty of worshipping emperor. Combined Judaism with Greek philosophy, particularly Platonism. Prolific writer on subjects connected with scripture and theology.

Pliny (the Younger) (around 61–113) Governor of Bithynia, where he had cause to ask the advice of the emperor Trajan regarding his policy towards Christianity. Famous for his letters and his eye-witness account of the eruption of Vesuvius.

Tertullian (around 160–225) Trained as a lawyer. Spent most of his life in Carthage. Most important for his ability to express Christian terms in Latin. Defended Christianity against pagans and Jews and expounded Christian doctrine and practice in the church. Later joined the strict Montanist sect.

Chapter 1

1 In many instances and many ways since long ago God has spoken to our fathers by the prophets, 2 and at the end of these days has spoken to us by his son, whom he has appointed heir of all, and through whom he made the ages, 3 and who, being a radiance of his glory and an expression of his being, and carrying all things by the word of his power, made a purification of sins and sat down at the right hand of the majesty in the heights.

[1] The opening phrase in Greek is **polymerôs kai polytropôs**. The AV translation, 'at sundry times and in divers manners', loses the repetition of **poly-**, but at least is more accurate than some modern versions which imply that God's message has been partial or piecemeal, or expressed in a fragmented way. Apart from the fact that the Greek words do not normally carry such meanings, there is a serious misunderstanding of the argument. The author is not saying that God's message in the past was somehow obscure or lacking, but rather that God has always and frequently made his message clear and now his own son has spoken directly to us. Indeed, there have been many occasions when God has spoken and he has used different approaches in order to express his meaning. Note, incidentally, that the word 'God' does not occur as first word in the passage.

Many translators have felt impelled to start with 'God . . .', but the writer knew that the alliteration and rhythm of the sentence would be better if 'God', **ho theos**, came later. The alliteration, *polymerôs kai polytropôs palai*, is echoed by Jerome in the Vulgate, *Multifariam multisque modis olim*.

[2] 'At the end of these days' recalls the Pauline idea not only that we are living at the end of this era, but also that the return of Christ in judgment is imminent. 'By his son', **en huiôi**, can also be translated 'in his son'. The expression 'through whom he made the ages' is echoed in the Nicene Creed's 'by whom all things were made'. Note that the word **aiôn** used here can mean 'world', 'eternity', 'epoch', or 'generation'. The well-known phrase 'world without end' translates the Greek **eis tous aiônas**, i.e. 'into the ages'.

[3] This verse is so rich in meanings that we should spend some time looking at the terms used. Firstly, **apaugasma**, translated here as 'radiance', is sometimes translated as 'reflection'. It occurs in the Wisdom of Solomon (7.26), where Wisdom is described as an **apaugasma** from the everlasting light. The image is that of a flash of light from a distant lighthouse or fire. A flash is a part of its source, while a reflection is a copy distinct from its original. The writer is saying that the Son shares the nature of the Father. This is reinforced in the next phrase, **charactêr tês hypostaseôs autou**, 'expression of his being'. A **charactêr** was the distinctive mark or impression left by a seal or die denoting ownership, and came to mean an image or exact copy which shares the nature or features of an original. **Hypostasis** is a complex word, literally, 'something settled beneath something else'. The Latin *substantia* or 'substance' is a translation of it. It can mean a 'sediment' or 'jelly', an 'essence', or denote the inner core or essential nature of a person. Here the writer is implying that the relationship

between the Son and the Father is so close that the one is the expression of the other, while remaining a distinct person.

Next we have **pherôn ta panta**, 'carrying all things'. This is deceptively simple. It can mean:

1. bringing to birth all things,
2. sustaining the universe (compare Colossians 1.17, 'and all things are held together by him'),
3. carrying all (our sins),
4. tolerating all (that we do),
5. bearing all (our sufferings),
6. bearing all (his pains), or
7. offering all the (necessary) offerings. In short, Jesus is creator, sustainer, scapegoat, friend, helper, victim and priest! If we have to choose, the second meaning seems most likely here.

'By the word of his power' can be expressed as 'by his powerful word'. The implication is that Jesus has the same power and authority as the Father, who says, 'Let there be light', and there is light. This is reinforced by the use of the term **rhêma**, not **logos**, the ordinary term for 'word'. **Rhêma** is the word of God expressing a creative act, i.e. the word as activity. A good example of this usage can be found in Luke's account of the Nativity (2.15–19) where the shepherds say, 'Let's go to Bethlehem and see *this word* (**rhêma**), *which has happened*, and which the Lord has made known to us.' And again, Mary 'kept all *these words* (**rhêmata**) in her heart and pondered them'. Note that in the AV **rhêma/rhêmata** is translated as 'thing(s)'.

4 He has been made so much greater than the angels, as the name he has inherited is so much more beyond them. 5 For to which of the angels did he ever say, 'You are my son; today I have begotten you', and again, 'I

shall be to him as a father and he will be to me as a son'?

[4] 'So much greater' refers to the glorification of the risen Christ which is alluded to in the previous verse, hence 'made' rather than 'born'. The name that Jesus has inherited is that of 'son'. Note 'inherited', not 'acquired', because he is already the son of God; it is not a reward for good conduct. The point of the argument is that, just as he is already superior to the angels because he was already the son of God, his incarnation, death and glorification have made him even more clearly superior to them.

Since it would be unthinkable for a strict Jew to allow God's divinity to be shared with another, Philo envisages the son of God as an angel: 'God's first born, the Word, who holds the eldership among the angels, an archangel, as it were' (*On the Confusion of Tongues*, 146). The writer probably has in mind Philo's statement and is anxious to re-define it in the light of the gospel.

[5] The texts quoted, from Ps. 2.7 and II Sam. 7.14, as Montefiore points out, seem to belong to a collection of rabbinical texts used for a different purpose. For instance, II Sam. 7.14 (AV) goes on to say, 'If he commit iniquity, I will chasten him with the rod of men and with the stripes of the children of men.' Although inappropriate in this passage, it could have been used in a Jewish context to refer to the Messiah.

6 And again, when he brings his first-born into the world, he says, 'and let all the angels of God bow before him.' 7 And in regard to his angels, he says, 'He who makes his angels winds and his ministers fiery

flame,' 8 and in regard to his son, 'Your throne, O God, is for ever and ever and the rod of righteousness is the rod of your kingdom. 9 You have loved justice and hated lawlessness; because of this, God, your God, has anointed you with the oil of joy beyond your fellows.' 10 And, 'You established, Lord, the earth in the beginning and the heavens are the work of your hands. 11 They will be destroyed, but you remain, and they will all grow old like a garment 12 and like a cloak, you will roll them up, and, like a garment, they will be changed. But you are the same and your years will not fail.'

[6] The reference to the angels worshipping Christ when he comes into the world is echoed by the nativity account of Luke (2.13–14).

'First-born', **prôtotokos**, implies seniority and, hence, superiority. The pre-existence of Christ before the incarnation is the underlying truth in this statement. The writer is not saying that Christ is the eldest of a series of sons, since the term 'first-born' frequently has an honorary sense in the Jewish scriptures. It is interesting, too, to note that the word translated here as 'world', **oikoumenê**, means literally 'the *inhabited* world'. In other words, the writer is seeing the incarnation as an event affecting mankind, not, in this context at least, as God entering the **kosmos**, the word most frequently used by such writers as Paul and John when referring to the incarnation.

The text here is taken from Ps. 97.7, which in the AV reads, 'worship him, all ye gods'. The author of this letter, however, is using the Septuagint version.

[7] The AV version of the text (Ps. 104. 4) is, 'Who maketh his

angels spirits; his ministers a flaming fire'. The Sept. version also refers to a flaming fire. We have a slight variation, 'flame of fire', but this is typical of someone quoting from memory rather than referring to a text. The significance of this text is that angels can be made and unmade, unlike the everlasting and unchanging son of God. Compare II (IV) Esdras 8.21–22 (NEB), 'who art attended by the host of angels trembling as they turn themselves into wind and fire at thy bidding'.

[8, 9] The reference here is to Ps. 45.6–7, again with minor variations from the Septuagint. The Greek for 'has anointed' is **echrisen**, which reminds us of the title of Jesus, **Christos**, the anointed one or the Messiah. An orthodox Jew would take the first verse as applying to God and the second to the Messiah, unless he took the first to mean, as it can in Greek, 'God *is* your throne . . . '

The writer, being a Christian, takes both verses as addressed to Jesus. Indeed, the Greek can be translated, 'O God, your God . . .' Psalm 45 also contains another Messianic reference, v. 2, which reads in the AV, 'Thou art fairer than the children of men; grace is poured into thy lips; therefore God hath blessed thee for ever.'

[10–12] The repetition, 'like a garment', is odd and is omitted in some manuscripts. These verses from Ps. 102.25–27 had already been taken as referring to the Messiah by pre-Christian scholars. Philo (*On Flight and Finding*, 110) speaks of the **kosmos** (defined as 'earth, water, air, fire,' etc.) as the robe of the **Logos**. The orthodox Jew would take the verses as applying to God.

13 And to which of the angels has he ever said, 'Sit at my right hand until I put your enemies beneath your

feet'? 14 Are they not all ministering spirits, sent out to serve for those who are to inherit salvation?

[13] Peter uses this text from Ps. 110.1 to show that the ascension of Jesus was foretold (Acts 2.34), and it underpins three other passages in the epistles of the NT: Rom. 8.34, Eph. 1.20 and Col. 3.1.

[14] This summarizes the argument. Angels are nothing more than the instruments of God, and their function is to serve him in his work of redemption. It is tempting to delete the word 'for', but the Greek does not allow it. The word translated here as 'for' is **dia**, which means 'on account of' or 'because of'. In other words, the angels do not serve us, but rather they assist God in fulfilling the scheme of salvation which is directed towards us.

Chapter 2

1 For this reason, we should pay greater attention to what we have heard, in case we should ever be negligent. 2 For if the word spoken by angels was reliable, and every transgression and disobedience received its due recompense, 3 how shall we escape, if we neglect such great salvation, which was first spoken of by the Lord, and then confirmed for us by those who heard him?

[1] Because the words for 'pay attention', **prosechein**, and 'be negligent', **pararrhein**, can also mean 'to moor' and 'to drift' respectively, William Barclay in his commentary on Hebrews introduces an interesting metaphor and translates this verse as, 'Therefore, we must the more eagerly anchor our lives to the things that we have been taught, lest the ship of life drift past the harbour and be wrecked.'

[2] The reference here is to the Law of Moses, which, according to tradition, was delivered by angels. Paul says (Gal. 3.19), 'So what about the Law? It was added because of transgressions, until such a time as the seed to whom the promise applied should come, and it was drawn up by means of angels at the hand of a mediator (i.e. Moses).' Paul is making a different point, since he is comparing the promise delivered

directly to Abraham with the commandments given by angels to Moses, who was himself a mediator, but the similarity is striking.

[3] The implication here is that the writer was not an original disciple of Jesus, but that he knew those who were. This again would fit in with what we know about Barnabas.

4 God, too, bears witness together with them, by signs and wonders and various acts of power and gifts of the Holy Spirit according to his own will. 5 For he did not subject to angels the world to come, the world of which we are speaking.

[4] In the original text this verse is a subordinate clause of the previous sentence, i.e. 'God, too, *bearing* witness . . .' Note that God is still working miracles and giving the gifts of the Holy Spirit, and this fact is further proof of the truth of the gospel.

The question is: with whom does God bear witness? Is it 'them', as suggested here, i.e. the original disciples, or is it 'him', i.e. the Lord Jesus? There is no pronoun in the Greek, so we have to make our own minds up on this matter. If we plump for 'them', we can take it as referring to the disciples *and* Jesus. The verb used here is **synepimartyreô**, 'I bear witness *with* (**syn-**) *in addition* (**epi-**).'

'Acts of power' are **dynameis**. The translation 'miracles' found in many versions, including the AV, unfortunately gives the impression that God's activity in the world is a violation of the natural order rather than a manifestation of the power of the Creator in his creation.

[5] 'The world to come' translates **tên oikoumenên tên**

mellousan. This is developed later in the letter, and is clearly the new Jerusalem, the true homeland of all believers. The paradox of the gospel is that this world is both 'to come' and already here now.

6 Somewhere someone has testified saying, 'What is man that you should remember him, or the son of man that you should consider him? 7 For a little while you have made him lower than the angels. You have crowned him with glory and honour. 8 You have subjected everything beneath his feet.' For, by subjecting everything to him, he has left nothing unsubjected. Yet we can see that everything is not yet subjected to him.

[6–8] The quotation is from Ps. 8.4–6 (omitting part of 6), which in the original is almost a hymn to the human state and the relationship human beings enjoy with God. Here the writer is treating the passage as Messianic, and the phrase 'son of man' refers to Christ. It continues the argument of ch. 1, namely, that Christ is superior to the angels.

[7] The alternative translation of **brachy ti**, 'for a little while', is '(a) little'; hence, 'you have made him little lower than the angels'. But this does not fit with v. 9, where it is clear that the writer is referring to the *temporary* subjection of Christ to death. It is inappropriate to say that Christ is nearly as high as an angel, when the main thrust of the argument is that he is higher than any angel but was temporarily humbled by his suffering death, so that we might share in the redemption brought about by that death.

Note the omission of part of v. 6 of the psalm quoted here, 'and established him over the works of your hands' (Sept.). This is in the original psalm from which this quotation is taken, and appears in several good manuscripts. It was probably added by later scholars when they compared the text with the original psalm, but it is likely that our writer left out this part because he was quoting from memory. Reliable early manuscripts do not include it.

[8] After his humiliation in death, Christ rises into glory. In this state he is Lord of all. But we can see that the world we live in seems not yet to be under his rule. The writer implies that it will be seen to be subjected to him, when he returns to claim his own.

9 And we can see that Jesus, who was made lower than the angels for a little while due to his suffering death, was crowned with glory and honour, so that, by the grace of God, he might taste death on everyone's behalf. 10 For since everything exists because of him and through him, it was right that he should make the perfect pioneer of their salvation through suffering the one leading many sons into glory.

[9] This is not an easy passage. The literal translation goes, 'We see the humiliated for a short time Jesus because of the suffering of death crowned with glory and honour . . .' It makes sense to take the phrase 'because of the suffering of death' with the first participle, 'humiliated', rather than the second, 'crowned'. The text, then, refers to Christ's death, resurrection and ascension. One can take the phrase 'crowned with glory and honour' as describing Christ's position before his incarnation, but it is unlikely in this context.

The next problem is a textual one. The phrase translated here as 'by the grace of God' is **chariti Theou**. There is an alternative reading, **chôris Theou,** meaning 'apart from God', found in various references in early scholars' works. The best manuscript reading, however, is **chariti**, followed by Jerome (Vulg. *gratia dei*). Some scholars who prefer **chôris** take the verse as saying that Christ tasted death for everyone apart from God, i.e. God did not need such a sacrifice. This appears unlikely and the more usual interpretation, by those who take this reading, of the phrase **chôris Theou** is that when Christ died for all he was separated from God, suffering alone the pains of death.

[10] The difficulty here is working out who is referred to in the phrases 'because of *him*' and 'through *him*' and who is the '*he*' in 'it was right that he . . .'. The grammar of the sentence leads us to treat the phrase 'leading many sons into glory' as describing Christ, and the phrase 'it was right that he . . .' as referring to the Father. Therefore, 'because of him' and 'through him' refer also to the Father. In other words, God the Father, who created all things, decided to make his son a perfect saviour through suffering, so that he might bring the human race into his kingdom as his own children. It is possible to take the verse as meaning, 'Jesus, through whom and because of whom everything exists, thought it right to make himself a perfect pioneer of salvation through suffering, etc.' The grammar, however, is against this interpretation, and Greek scholars such as Chrysostom, writing towards the end of the fourth century, clearly take the Father as the subject of this sentence.

In his *Homilies on Hebrews* Chrysostom says on this text, 'He has done what is worthy of his love towards mankind, in showing his first-born to be more glorious than all, and in setting him forth as an example to others, like some noble wrestler that surpasses the rest.'

The expression 'make perfect', **teleiôsai**, needs some explanation. This verb in Greek does not mean 'to make perfect something which is imperfect', but rather has the sense of 'completing' or 'bringing to maturity'. See the note on 5.9.

11 For he who sanctifies, and those who are sanctified, are all from the one [father], and for this reason he is not ashamed to call them brothers 12 saying, 'I shall announce your name to my brothers; in the midst of the assembly I will sing your praise.' 13 And again, 'I shall trust in him', and again, 'behold, I and the children whom God gave me'.

[11] Jesus is the sanctifier; we are the sanctified. We have one Father, so we are the brothers (and sisters) of Jesus. A new relationship has been established. The New English Bible inexplicably alters 'them' to 'men', and translates the last part of this verse as, 'he does not shrink from calling men his brothers'. This changes a statement about the personal relationship between Jesus and the believer into a general observation about Jesus' attitude towards the whole of mankind.

[12] This verse is from Psalm 22 (v. 22), a psalm full of Messianic texts. It is in this psalm that we find the last words of Jesus, 'My God, my God, why have you forsaken me?'

[13] The reference here is to Isa. 8.17–18, quoting from the Sept. (hence 'I shall *trust* in him') with a slight variation of the word order. In the AV, v. 17 reads in full, 'And I will wait upon the Lord, that hideth his face from the house of Jacob, and I will *look for* him.' The variation in word order is another indication that our writer is quoting from memory rather than a written text. The ability to carry numerous texts in one's memory is common in societies where books are not readily or cheaply available for the average person. We can easily forget

how remarkable is the human capacity to retain long texts in the memory.

14 So, since the children have shared flesh and blood, he, too, has participated equally in the same, so that he might abolish through his death the one who has the power of death, namely, the devil, 15 and set free those who by fear of death were throughout life liable to be slaves. 16 For to be sure, he does not lay hold of angels, but the seed of Abraham. 17 Hence it was necessary that he should be like his brothers in all points, so that he might be a merciful and faithful high priest in their dealings with God for the expiation of the sins of his people. 18 For in that he was tested and suffered himself, he can help those being tested.

[14] 'Have shared', **kekoinônêken**, has the sense of sharing *in common*. 'To share *as an* individual' is **metechein**, which is the verb translated here as 'participated'. We are reminded of the sharing of blood and flesh in communion or fellowship, **koinôniâ**. The point here is that by taking on flesh, Christ shared with us the human condition. This involved suffering, and indeed one manuscript adds 'suffering' after 'the same'.

The connection between the devil and death is familiar in traditional Jewish thought. It was believed that God did not create death and that it was through the devil that death entered the world (Wisdom of Solomon 1.13 and 2.23–24). The Christian answer is given in Rev. 1.17–18, 'Fear not. I am the first and the last and the living one; I was dead and, look, I am alive for ever and ever, and I hold the keys of death and Hades.'

[15] 'Slaves', that is, of death and sin.

[16] 'Lay hold of', **epilambanetai,** needs some explanation. Christ did not take on the nature of angels but of humankind. This meant that he seized and occupied the human body. Chrysostom gives this interpretation and goes on to develop the idea as follows: 'It is derived from the figure of persons pursuing those who turn away from them, and doing everything to overtake them as they flee, and to take hold of them, as they are bounding away.' Recently it has become acceptable to take **epilambanetai** as meaning 'he assists (or helps)'. Apart from the fact that the verb cannot carry this meaning, it misses the point of the passage, which is that Christ took on our flesh and did not stand apart from us. He became a man, not an angel.

[17] The writer sums up the previous argument and adds a new idea, that by sharing our nature, Christ was able to act as an effective high priest on our behalf, so that our relationship with the Father might be restored. This is developed in the next chapter.

[18] The verb 'to be tested', **peirâsthai,** is often translated as 'to be tempted', but this tends to be taken in a narrow sense. Temptation is only part of the testing, trials and tribulations which are summed up by the noun **peirâsmos.**

Chapter 3

1 Therefore, holy brothers and sisters, sharers in the heavenly calling, consider the envoy and high priest of our confession, Jesus, 2 faithful to the one who appointed him, as Moses also was in all his household. 3 For he has been reckoned more worthy of honour than Moses, in so far as the one who has established the household has more honour than the household. 4 For every household is established by someone, and he who has established everything is God.

[1] 'Envoy', **apostolos**, corresponds here to the Hebrew *shaliach*, an authorized representative of a community, literally, 'one who is sent', rather than 'apostle', which denotes someone 'sent out' to preach the gospel. In a Jewish context, therefore, an **apostolos** is sent by the people to God, i.e. as a mediator or representative.

Note also the word translated here as 'confession', **homologiâ**. This is an agreement, a contract or compact. It describes the faith and doctrine we profess. There is a passage in Matthew (10.32) where the verb **homologeô** is used in precisely this sense: 'Everyone who confesses (**homologêsei**) me before men, I will confess (**homologêsô**) before my Father in heaven.'

[2] The word 'all' is omitted in many manuscripts, but appears

in some early ones, and is part of the original text from which it comes, Num. 12.7. It is quoted again with 'all' in v. 5 of this chapter.

[3] 'Honour', **doxa**, is more often translated as 'glory', but that would not fit here.

Why does the writer, having established that Jesus is superior to the angels, need to prove that he is also superior to Moses? Because Moses was regarded as superior to the angels. Rabbi Jose ben Chalafta says, 'God calls Moses faithful in all his house, and thereby ranked him higher than the ministering angels themselves.' The Numbers passage quoted here speaks of the difference between Moses and other prophets. Verse 8 goes on to say, 'With him will I speak mouth to mouth', in contrast to other prophets to whom God speaks in dreams or visions.

'The one who has established the household' is Jesus, who, being God, is the creator of the household of Moses, i.e. Israel.

[4] This reinforces the previous verse, i.e. Jesus is God.

5 And, 'Moses was faithful in his whole household as a servant'; this was as a testimony to what would be spoken. 6 But Christ is over his household as a son, whose household we are, if we continue steadfast, speaking freely and proclaiming our hope until the end.

[5] 'What would be spoken' is most probably a reference to God's message on Sinai.

[6] Christ differs from Moses, because he created the household of Moses. Now we have a second difference: Moses was

merely a servant, whereas Christ is the son of the Lord of the household. We are reminded of the parable of the wicked husbandmen, to whom the landlord sends his servants to collect his revenues, and after they were badly treated, sends his own son.

The AV 'if we hold fast the confidence and the rejoicing of the hope firm unto the end' seems almost to point to a private acceptance of the gospel. This is true also of some more modern translations, such as the New International Version, 'if we hold onto our courage and the hope of which we boast'. But the writer is referring to open confession of the faith, not some internal assent. There are two Greek words used here that are frequently mistranslated, **parrhêsiâ** and **kauchêma**. Firstly, **parrhêsia** is often used by Paul to express our new relationship with God, i.e. we can speak freely with him, and thus tends to be translated as 'confidence'. But the central meaning of **parrhêsiâ** is 'free speech', i.e. 'speaking freely and openly before others'. This can be illustrated from Eph. 6.19, 'so that I might be given the power to open my mouth and speak and make known with boldness (**en parrhêsiâi**) the mystery of the gospel'. Similarly, **kauchêma**, and its associated verb, **kauchâsthai**, besides meaning 'boast', frequently have the sense 'speak loudly about', or 'proclaim openly'.

The theme running through this letter to the Hebrews is one of confessing the faith openly. When the writer exhorts his audience, he does not tell them to cultivate their faith in secret, but rather to proclaim it to the world. Incidentally, some manuscripts leave out 'steadfast' and 'until the end', probably because the same words occur in v. 14.

7 Therefore, as the Holy Spirit says, 'Today, if you hear his voice, 8 do not harden your hearts, as in the rebellion in the day of temptation in the wilderness, 9 when your fathers tempted and tested me and saw my

works 10 for forty years; therefore, I was angry with this generation and said, "They are always wrong in their hearts; they have not known my ways", 11 as I swore in my anger that they should not enter my rest.'

[7–11] Psalm 95.7–11: the 'rebellion' is probably the one described in Numbers 20, when the Israelites complained about a shortage of water. Moses showed his disobedience when God told him to speak to the rock in order to procure water, and instead he struck the rock. As a result God punished Moses by not allowing him to enter the promised land. This is the third difference between Christ and Moses: Moses was unfaithful and disobedient.

[10] 'For forty years' has been detached by our writer from the following sentence and taken with the previous one. This does not materially affect the sense. Instead of saying that God was angry for forty years, our text states that they saw God's works for forty years. Some see the forty years as pointing to the interval between the death of Jesus and the fall of Jerusalem. This would force us to put the date of the composition of this letter to some time after 70, the date of the fall, if, indeed, it could be proved that this allusion was intended.

[11] Rabbi Akiba (died AD 132) took the verse in the psalm as signifying that the whole generation of guilty Israelites was excluded from the world to come. Rabbi Eliezer (circa AD 100) took a gentler line and said that God later withdrew his oath.

What is meant by 'rest'? In the original account it signifies the reaching of the promised land, but soon takes on a deeper meaning. Because the Lord rested on the seventh day, and that was a day without end, the Lord's rest was seen as eternal.

Hence, those who enter his rest enter eternity. For the writer, our attainment of this rest depends on our obedience.

12 Watch out, brothers and sisters, lest there be in any of you a wicked heart of disbelief and rebellion against the living God. 13 But encourage one another every day, while it is called 'today', so that none of you become hardened by the deceitfulness of sin. 14 For we have become sharers in Christ, if we keep unshaken the original foundation until the end. 15 As the saying goes, 'Today, if you hear his voice, do not harden your hearts as in the rebellion.'16 For who listened but rebelled? Surely it was all those who came out of Egypt through Moses?

[12] **Apistiâ**, 'disbelief', 'disobedience', and its opposite **pistis**, 'obedience', 'faithfulness' (often translated 'faith'), are the recurrent theme throughout this letter.

[14] 'The original foundation', **tên archên tês hypostaseôs**, literally, 'the start of the underlying part'. See note on 1.3 for **hypostasis**.

[15] A repeat of part of Ps. 95.7,8.

[16] For reasons of style and grammar, this verse, like the following ones, is best taken as a question; 'surely it was' = 'was it not?'

17 With whom was he angry for forty years? Was it not those who had sinned, whose limbs fell in the desert? 18 And to whom did he swear that they would

not enter his rest, if it was not to those who had been disobedient? 19 Indeed we can see that they could not enter because of their faithlessness.

[17] The coupling of 'forty years' with 'he was angry' is the usual form of the text of the quotation: see the note on v. 10. For an understanding of this passage, see Num. 14.29–33.

[18] This is a reference to the disobedient Israelites including Moses. 'Disobedient' here is from the verb **apeitheô**, opposite of **peithomai**, 'I obey'.

[19] The writer skilfully sums up and at the same time points forward to the theme of the next chapter. For 'faithlessness', **apistiâ**, see the note on v. 12.

Chapter 4

1 Let us, therefore, be afraid lest, while there remains a promise of entering his rest, any of you should be seen to have lost it. 2 For, indeed, we have been given the good news, just as they have, but the report they heard did not help them, since they were not stirred by belief in those who had heard.

[1] 'Have lost it', from **hystereô**, literally, 'fall behind', hence, 'come too late' or 'fail'.

[2] This is not an easy verse, due to the subtle allusions and layers of meaning, and it has been made more difficult by textual problems. Firstly, 'just as they have' is generally taken as referring to the Jews who did not accept the reports of the spies on the land of Canaan (Numbers 13 and 14). But it is also possible to take it as referring to those Jews who had rejected the gospel of Christ. 'The report they heard', **logos tês akoês**, literally, 'the word of hearing', Vulg. *sermo auditus*, is almost a synonym for 'gospel'. I Thess. 2.13 has the same phrase: 'when you received the **logon akoês** of God from us, you welcomed it, not as a human message, but as God's message, which is what it truly is'.

The text at this point has several variations, which would take some time to explain. The most likely is one that reads 'since they were not stirred (literally, 'mingled with', **syng-kekrasmenous**) by belief *in those who had heard*, **tois akousâsin**'. 'Those who had heard' are either those who believed the good reports about Canaan, i.e. Moses and Aaron, or, if we take the verse as referring to the Christian gospel, the disciples who were eye-witnesses of Jesus and who had heard the gospel from him directly. See 2.3 for the same use of this expression: 'and then confirmed for us *by those who heard him*, **hypo tôn akousantôn**'. the implication is that the persons addressed by our writer had originally been evangelized by preachers who had heard and seen Christ in the flesh.

3 For we who have believed do enter his rest; as he has said, 'As I swore in my anger, they will not enter my rest', and, furthermore, [the rest] from the labours which took place at the foundation of the world. 4 For he has said this somewhere regarding the seventh day, 'And God rested on the seventh day from all his labours', 5 and on the same subject again, 'they will not enter my rest'.

[3] The writer quotes again from Ps. 95.11.

'And furthermore', **kaitoi**, which some attempt to translate as 'although', but with little justification. The omission of 'the rest' is typical of Greek prose. The meaning of the verse is quite clear: non-believers do not gain the eternal rest established by God at the first sabbath, but believers do. See the note on 3.11. The rabbis thought it significant that the account in Genesis of the Creation tells us that every day had an evening and a morning except the seventh, which was the day God rested. Therefore, God's rest is eternal.

[4, 5] The writer quotes from Gen. 2.2, clearly from memory,

as we see throughout this letter, and repeats yet again part of the verse from Ps.95. His main theme is that eternal life can only be attained by faithfulness, and he stresses the parallel between the situation of the Israelites in the desert, and that of the Jewish Christians facing persecution in his own day.

6 So, since it is left open for some to enter it, and since those who first received the good news did not enter because of their disbelief, 7 he ordains again a day, that is, today, speaking in [the psalm of] David, after so long a time, as the prophecy goes: 'Today, if you hear his voice, do not harden your hearts.' 8 For if Joshua (Jesus) had given them rest, he would not be speaking of another day afterwards. 9 So there is still left the sabbath for the people of God. 10 For someone who has entered his peace, has also ceased from his labours, as God did from his. 11 Let us, therefore, strive to enter that rest, lest anyone fall in the same pattern of faithlessness.

[6–11] This passage again is generally taken as referring to the disobedient Israelites but it can be taken as reflecting the situation facing the writer's audience. Some who received the gospel have abandoned it and lost their hope of entering into eternal rest. The sabbath of the people of God remains as a goal to be attained by the faithful. Commentators who treat this passage simply as applicable to the Jews of the exodus, interpret the **Iêsous** of v. 8 only as a reference to Joshua. The name, of course, is the same as 'Jesus'. The coincidence certainly would have struck the audience.

[6] 'Disbelief', **apeitheia**, is translated as 'faithlessness' in v.

11. In English we have no single word which conveys the sense of **pistis**, or of its opposite, **apistiâ** or **apeitheia**. **Pistis** is not only the intellectual assent conveyed by our word 'belief', but also the faithfulness of an obedient disciple. See the note on 11.6.

[7] 'After so long a time' refers to the time elapsing between the events described in Numbers and the date of the composition of the Psalms. 'As the prophecy goes', **kathôs proeirêtai**, could also be translated, 'as has been spoken of beforehand'. The rest prophesied for the people of God has still to be achieved. 'Today' is the day of the Lord, the eternal sabbath which is his present, as well as our present time, when we can still repent.

'He' in this verse is God speaking through the scriptures. The meaning of this verse, if we believe that it applies to Joshua, is that even when he and the faithful Israelites had reached the promised land, he could not give them the rest of the eternal sabbath. If we take the verse as referring to Jesus, the meaning is that our Lord did not give his followers the final rest. That peace is still to come and will be attained fully by the faithful when they enter heaven.

[9, 10] **Sabbatismos**, a word found nowhere else in the Bible, is translated here as 'the Sabbath', but really means 'following the practices of the Sabbath' or 'living a Sabbath life'. It is the state attained by those who enter the eternal rest of God. This cannot be reached before we cease from our labours.

[11] 'The pattern of faithlessness' could be the example of disobedience provided by the Israelites who were deprived of the rest promised to those who obeyed the Lord, or that provided by the apostate Jewish Christians referred to above.

12 For the word of God is alive and active, sharper than any two–edged sword, and piercing to the separation of soul and spirit, of joints and marrow, and able to scrutinize the thoughts and designs of the heart. 13 And there is no creature hidden before him, but all is naked and stripped bare to the eyes of the one with whom we have to reckon.

[12] Chrysostom took 'the word' (**logos**) to refer to Christ, but it is probable that the writer is referring to the word of God expressed through his prophets. The texts on which this imagery is probably based could support either hypothesis. Wisdom of Solomon 18.15–16 (NEB) describes the Word in a similar way: '. . . when thy almighty Word leapt from thy royal throne in heaven into the midst of that doomed land like a relentless warrior, bearing the sharp sword of thy inflexible decree . . .' On the other hand, Isa. 49.2 describes the prophet as saying (AV), 'And he hath made my mouth like a sharp sword'.

'Soul and spirit', **psûchê**, the animal life-force or breath of life, and **pneuma**, the spiritual core of a person. The 'separation' of the two probably does not refer to the process of dying but rather signifies that God can penetrate the innermost recesses of the personality and consequently nothing is hidden from him. This leads on to a reference to the final judgment of God, 'with whom we have to reckon', **pros hon hêmîn ho logos**, which we can also translate as, 'before whom we have to plead'. **Logos** here means 'account'. This allusion to judgment is reinforced by 'able to scrutinize', **kritikos**, from the word for 'judge', **kritês**.

[13] 'Stripped bare', **tetrachêlismena**, literally, 'having the neck twisted', Vulg. *aperta*, 'open(ed)'. This has been interpreted in various ingenious ways, but Chrysostom probably gives

the correct definition: 'It is a metaphor from the skins which are drawn off from the victims. For as in that case, when a man has killed them and has drawn aside the skin from the flesh, he lays open all the inward parts, and makes them manifest to our eyes; so also do all things lie open before God.' The verb **trachêlizô** was used to describe the act of twisting the neck of a sacrificial victim, then probably was extended to describe the act of butchering. Hence a carcass hung up in a butcher's shop would be described as **tetrachêlismenos**. I was recently forcibly reminded of this when visiting the Turkish market in Nicosia, Cyprus. The internal organs or offal of a butchered animal were displayed suspended from the neck of the carcass within the body cavity. 'All is naked and stripped bare . . .'

14 So, having a great high priest who has penetrated the heavens, Jesus the son of God, let us keep hold of our confession. 15 For we do not have a high priest incapable of suffering with us in our sicknesses, but one who has been tested in all respects like us, except in the matter of sinfulness. 16 Let us, therefore, approach with confidence the throne of grace, so that we may receive mercy and find grace to help us in season.

[14] 'Penetrated' carries on the same imagery of the 'piercing' word and supports Chrysostom's interpretation of the previous passage as referring to Christ. The theme of the high priest will be developed in the next chapter.

[15] 'Sicknesses', **astheneiais**, literally 'weaknesses', including 'illnesses', and 'ailments'. It is not necessary here to take the word in a moral sense. 'Tested', **pepeirâsmenon**; see the note on 2.18.

[16] 'With confidence', **meta parrhêsiâs**; but see the note on 3.6.

Chapter 5

1 For every high priest taken from mankind is ordained on behalf of mankind in matters relating to God, so that he may offer gifts and sacrifices for sins, 2 being able to treat the ignorant and those who are going astray with fairness, since he, too, is invested with weakness. 3 And because of this he must make his offering also for himself as well as for the people in regard to sins. 4 And one does not take the honour for oneself, but is called by God, as Aaron also was.

[1–4] The background for this and subsequent references to the high priest is the ritual followed by the Jews on the Day of Atonement. It is significant that the plural phrase **hyper hamartiôn**, 'for sins', is only used in the Septuagint to refer to this occasion.

[2] 'To treat . . . with fairness', **metriopathein**, needs some explanation. Philo (*On Abraham*, 44) uses this verb to describe the mean between extravagant grief and stoic apathy in reference to Abraham's sorrow for his wife's death. But Josephus (*Antiquities*, XII 128) uses it to describe the moderation shown by Vespasian and Titus in their treatment of the Jews after the war in Judaea which began in 66. This is the sense it carries in this passage; the high priest is required to be

neither over-indulgent nor hypercritical. This is because he is as much a sinner as those on whose behalf he ministers. The statement 'he is invested with weakness', **perikeitai astheneian**, is not to be taken as implying that he is merely aware of human weakness. Nor should we assume this description applies to Christ.

[3] It is clear that the need of the high priest to sacrifice for his own sins as well as the people's is due to the fact that he is a sinner. 'And *because of this*', i.e. 'weakness', he must sacrifice on his own behalf. We can see later (7.28) that the writer contrasts the weakness of the high priests with the perfection of the son.

[4] The choice of Aaron by God is a reference to Ex. 28.1. In order to preserve the symmetry of the comparison of the earthly high priest with Christ, the writer has not mentioned that God chose Aaron *and* his sons.

5 So Christ also did not glorify himself in being made a high priest but the one who said to him, 'You are my son; today I have begotten you', glorified him. 6 As he says also in another place, 'You are a priest for ever according to the order of Melchizedek.' 7 In the days of his incarnation, when he had offered prayers and intercessions with loud cries and tears to the one who could save from death, although he was heard because of his piety, 8 despite being his son, he learned from his sufferings obedience, 9 and being made perfect, he became the cause of everlasting salvation to all who obey him, 10 being called by God High Priest according to the order of Melchizedek.

[5] John 1.14, 'and we have seen his glory, the glory of the only-begotten of his Father', explains this verse: Christ's glory was due to the fact that he was God's son. The quotation is from Psalm 2.7, previously quoted in 1.5 of this letter.

[6] The reference is to Psalm 110.4. The significance of the reference to Melchizedek is made clear in Chapter 7.

[7] The reference is to the sufferings of Christ in Gethsemane. 'Although he was heard because of his piety', **eisakoustheis apo tês eulabeiâs**, is rendered by Montefiore as 'being heard (he was set free) from fear'. There is nothing here which corresponds to 'he was set free', and the word translated by Montefiore as 'fear' is rarely used in this sense. **Eulabeia** is godly fear, the awe felt by a pious disciple towards God. Christ's prayer that the cup should be taken away was not *granted*. This does not mean that his prayer was not *heard*.

[8] This verse can be misunderstood; on the surface it implies that Christ had not been obedient and had to suffer in order to learn obedience. The confusion arises from the fact that we have here a proverbial expression, **emathen aph' hôn epathen**, which expresses the familiar truth that there is no substitute for experience. In other words, unless you have really experienced something you do not know much about it. Christ knew what obedience was; what he experienced now was the consequence of his obedience. In Greek literature we frequently meet the saying **pathos mathos**, 'suffering is learning', but it is a stronger expression than it would appear to us. In Greek tragedy the victim neither learns some philosophic truth, nor becomes a better person, through suffering, but rather learns what suffering is.

[9] 'Being made perfect', **teleiôtheis**, Vulg. *consummatus*, does

not mean that some moral imperfection was corrected, but rather that Christ's work of redemption was completed; he became fully the man that his incarnation meant he should be by experiencing all that humanity experiences in suffering and death. See the note on 'make perfect' in 2.10.

[10] 'Called', i.e. addressed as such by God, **prosagoreutheis**, not 'called' in the sense of a vocational calling.

11 Of him I have much to say, and it is a subject difficult to put into words, since you are slow learners. 12 For indeed, although you ought to be teachers because of your experience, you need to be taught again the basic principles of God's word and you need milk not solid food. 13 For everyone who takes milk is inexperienced in the meaning of righteousness, for he is an infant. 14 But adults have solid food, that is, those who have their senses habitually trained to discern good and evil.

[11] 'Difficult to put into words', **dysermêneutos**, i.e. 'hard to interpret'.

[12] 'Because of your experience', **dia ton chronon**, literally, 'because of the time', referring to the lapse of time since they had first heard the gospel or since they first studied the scriptures.

'The basic principles of God's word', **ta stoicheia tês archês tôn logiôn tou Theou**, literally, 'the elements of the beginning of the sayings of God'. This must refer to their understanding of the scriptures. The writer is asking them to look again at the crucial texts which speak of Christ and his work of redemption.

[13] 'Inexperienced in the meaning of righteousness', **apeiros logou dikaiosynês,** is not an easy phrase to interpret. We can discard such translations as 'incapable of accurate self-expression', or 'incapable of understanding normal adult language', because they do not reflect the meaning of **dikaiosynê,** 'righteousness' or 'justice', nor does the translation 'without experience of moral truth' reflect the reference to scripture implied in **logos,** 'word' or 'account'. There is some justification in translating this phrase as 'unacquainted with the righteousness of God revealed in Christ', because **logos** can refer to the divine Word, but it fits the context better if we take it as meaning something like 'unacquainted with the teaching of righteousness found in scripture'. One activity of God is the exercise of his **dikaiosynê,** and the scriptures give an account of this.

[14] 'Adults', **teleioi,** 'mature people', literally, 'completed' (Vulg. *perfecti).*

Chapter 6

1 Therefore, let us leave behind the elementary gospel of Christ, and make for maturity and not lay down again the foundation of repentance from dead works and of belief in God, 2 of the teaching of baptism, and of the laying on of hands, of the resurrection of the dead, and of everlasting judgment. 3 This is what we shall do, if God allows us.

[1] 'The elementary gospel', **ton tês archês tou Christou logon**, literally, 'the account of the beginning of Christ'.

'Dead works' are 'sins', as in 9.14, not the 'works of the law'. It is unnecessary to introduce here any reference to Paul's argument in his letter to the Romans.

[2] 'The laying on of hands' could be connected with the ceremony of baptism or other Christian practices such as the healing of the sick or ordination.

4 For it is impossible for those who have once seen the light, tasted the heavenly gift and become participators in the Holy Spirit, 5 and who have tasted the good word of God and the powers of the world to come, 6 once they have fallen away, to renew their repentance

again by crucifying for themselves anew the son of God and making a spectacle of him. 7 For the earth that drinks the rain that often falls on it and produces suitable crops for those who till it, receives a blessing from God. 8 But if it bears thistles and thorns, it is rejected and comes close to being cursed and its end is to be burned.

[4] 'Seen the light', **phôtisthentas,** or 'illuminated', is often used in the early church to describe the baptized. It certainly indicates here those who have received the Holy Spirit and is used again in this sense in 10.32.

'Impossible', **adynaton,** has been a source of comment. Attempts have been made to soften the harshness of this passage by interpreting the word as meaning merely 'difficult'. For the early church, however, re-admitting lapsed Christians was often regarded as impossible.

[5] 'The good word', **kalon rhêma,** is not the **logos** or message of the gospel but some solemn pronouncement, say, at baptism. See note on 1.3.

'The powers of the world to come', **dynameis mellontos aiônos,** are the gifts of the Spirit, who has equipped us for our new life in heaven. We are no longer citizens of this material world but of the new Jerusalem. Chrysostom says cryptically of these powers that they are 'life eternal; angelic conversation'. These are not only to be made manifest in the future; they operate now. The world to come is already at work.

[6] 'Making a spectacle of', **paradeigmatizontas,** originally 'making an example of', hence 'exposing to public shame'. If an apostate attempts to return to the church that he has rejected he brings Christ into disrepute. By renewing their vows they are in

a sense crucifying Christ again. When we read in Pliny's letter to Trajan of the measures he had taken to combat Christianity (Book 10, letter 96), we can see that the act of renouncing Christianity was a public spectacle that was calculated to insult Christ, '*Omnes et imaginem tuam deorumque simulacra venerati sunt; et Christo maledixerunt*' – 'They all worshipped your statue and the images of the gods; and cursed Christ.' It is tempting to assume that our writer is describing the act of apostasy itself rather than the attempt of the apostate to return to the church, but it is clear from the present tense of two participles used in this verse (**anastaurountas**, 'crucifying anew', and **paradeigmatizontas**), that he is referring to the latter.

Some scholars take **anastaurountas** simply as 'crucifying', but Jerome translates it as 'crucifying anew', *rursum crucifigentes*. This is supported by Chrysostom, who argues that as our first baptism was a cross on which our old self was crucified with Christ, we would be attempting to crucify him again if we tried to return after apostasy. Chrysostom seems to think that there would be a need for a second baptism, but it is extremely unlikely that he would have allowed such a practice, and we must assume he is speaking hypothetically.

[7, 8] An echo of Gen. 3.17, 18 (AV), 'cursed is the ground for thy sake; in sorrow shalt thou eat of it all the days of thy life; thorns also and thistles shall it bring forth to thee'. One is also reminded of the parable of the tares (Matt. 13.24–30), and of the sower (Matt. 13.3–8; Mark 4.3–8; Luke 8.5–8). Both these parables have a direct bearing on the subject of lapsed Christians. Our writer seems to be aware of the harshness of his message and goes on to address his audience in a more conciliatory tone.

9 But even if we speak in this way, we are persuaded,

beloved, to believe better of you and that you are holding on to salvation. 10 For God is not so unfair as to forget your labour and the love you have shown his name, as you have served and are still serving his saints. 11 We yearn for each of you to show the same eagerness towards the fulfilment of your hope until the end, 12 so that you may be not sluggish but imitators of those who inherit the promises through faith and patience.

[9] 'And that you are holding on to salvation', **kai echomena sôtêriâs**, literally, 'and that which is holding on to salvation'. This rather oblique expression shows that our writer is avoiding saying outright that they are safe. He wants to soften the tone of his previous lecture, but not too much.

[10] This verse with its distinction between 'have served' and 'serving', **diâkonêsantes** and **diâkonountes**, probably refers to the good record of the people he is addressing in welcoming apostles and evangelists. Montefiore sees a possible reference here to their having given aid to the church in Jerusalem.

[12] Those who 'inherit the promises through faith and patience' are probably Christians who stand firm in times of persecution and suffer for their faith. The implication is that this audience knew many such personally.

13 For, when God made his promises to Abraham, he swore by himself, since he had no other greater to swear by, 14 saying, 'Surely in blessing I will bless you and in increasing I will increase you.' 15 And by being patient in this way Abraham won the promise. 16 For

human beings swear by something greater [than themselves], and an oath acts as a guarantee and a final decision in every dispute with them. 17 In this matter God, wishing to make absolutely clear to the heirs of the promise the unalterable nature of his will, intervened with an oath, 18 so that through two unalterable matters, where God could not lie, we who have fled to him for refuge should have a firm encouragement to lay hold of the hope that lies before us, 19 and which we have as a firm and sure anchor of the soul, and which enters into the innermost part beyond the veil, 20 where Jesus entered as a forerunner for us, having become a high priest for ever according to the order of Melchizedek.

[13–18] The key text for an understanding of this passage is Gen. 22.16–18, which reads in the AV, 'By myself have I sworn, saith the Lord, for because thou hast done this thing, and hast not withheld thy son, thine only son: that in blessing I will bless thee, and in multiplying I will multiply thy seed as the stars of the heaven, and as the sand which is upon the sea shore; and thy seed shall possess the gate of his enemies; and in thy seed shall all the nations of the earth be blessed; because thou hast obeyed my voice.'

Philo (*Allegory of the Laws*, 3.203), echoing the rabbis, comments on God's oath by himself; 'for there is nothing better than He', **ouden gar autou kreitton**.

[18] The 'two unalterable matters' are either the two promises of (a) the new land mentioned in Gen. 12.1, and (b) the fathering of many nations mentioned in Gen. 17.4–6, or, as seems more likely, the two promises recalled above in v. 14,

'Surely in blessing I will bless you, and in increasing I will increase you'. It has also been suggested that the two unalterable matters are, firstly, that he promised, and secondly, that he swore by himself.

[19] The anchor soon became a familiar emblem of the Christian hope, and there is no doubt that 'hope' is the subject of v. 19 rather than the 'encouragement' mentioned earlier.

'The veil' is the hanging, **katapetasma**, in the Temple which separated the Holy of Holies from the rest of the shrine, but is used here to signify the heavenly veil which Christ penetrated when he had offered the sacrifice of himself to God. This double layer of meaning is typical of our writer and, indeed, of traditional rabbinical argument, in which it would be common to expound an allegorical or inner meaning having first carefully defined the apparent meaning.

[20] 'Forerunner', **prodromos**, echoes the description of Christ as a pioneer, **archêgos**, in 2.10.

Chapter 7

1 For this Melchizedek, king of Salem, priest of the most high God, met Abraham returning from the killing of the kings and blessed him, 2 and Abraham gave him a tenth of everything as a tithe. Firstly, his name when interpreted means 'King of Righteousness', and secondly, he was 'King of Salem', that is, 'King of Peace', 3 being without father or mother, with no record of ancestors, having no beginning of days or end of life, and who, being made like the Son of God, remains a priest in perpetuity.

[1] The incident referred to here is described in Gen. 14.18–20. A detail is omitted by our writer, which has led to comment. Verse 18 of the Genesis account mentions that Melchizedek 'brought forth bread and wine'. Some conclude from this omission that our writer could hardly have had the eucharist in mind while writing this epistle. It is just as likely that the omission was due to the fact that the eucharist was a sacred mystery and not a matter to be spoken of openly on this occasion. It is also possible that he deliberately leaves it out because it is alluded to later in 13.10. It is even more likely that the reason for the omission is that it was not relevant to mention the bread and wine, since our writer is only interested here in those details that establish the inferiority of Abraham to Melchizedek.

The fact that Melchizedek blessed Abraham is significant. It shows that he is Abraham's superior.

[2] Titles such as 'king of righteousness' and 'king of peace' clearly have a Messianic significance, as we can see when we read Isa. 9.6–7 (AV), '. . . and his name shall be called . . . the Prince of Peace. Of the increase of his government and peace there shall be no end, upon the throne of David, and upon his kingdom, to order it, and to establish it with judgment and with justice from henceforth even for ever . . .'

The fact that Abraham pays tithes is significant: Jews paid tithes to their own priests but Melchizedek was not a priest as far as Abraham was concerned and so tithing would not normally have been appropriate. Abraham's payment of tithes shows that he recognised that Melchizedek did in fact have a special claim on him.

[3] 'With no record of ancestors', **agenealogêtos,** because nowhere in scripture is the family of Melchizedek mentioned. The writer also points out that we have no record of his birth or death. Consequently he is an everlasting priest. 'In perpetuity', **eis to diênekes,** not 'continually', as in the AV, since the meaning of this word has changed since the seventeenth century, but 'continuously' or 'for ever'.

'Being made like the Son of God', i.e. he is the type of Christ, or he can be compared with him. It would be irrelevant to ask whether our writer believed that Melchizedek was a real figure representing Christ or that he actually was Christ. His main concern is to demonstrate that Christ was prophesied in scripture; as he says at the start of the letter, God has spoken about him in the prophets.

The writer has established that Melchizedek/Christ is superior to Abraham. He will now demonstrate that he is also

superior to the traditional priest who according to the law of
Moses had to be descended from Levi.

4 Consider how important this man is, to whom the
patriarch Abraham gave a tenth of the spoils. 5 And
the sons of Levi, on the one hand, when they take on
their priesthood, have a commandment that they
should tithe the people according to the law, that is,
their brothers, even though they are direct descendants
of Abraham. 6 But on the other hand, the one who has
no ancestor of theirs has tithed Abraham and blessed
the one possessing the promises. 7 Beyond all con-
tradiction, the lesser is blessed by the greater. 8 And on
one hand, here it is mortals who receive tithes, but
there it is someone acknowledged to be alive.

[4] 'Patriarch' has the sense here of 'founder of the race'.
Abraham is the father of the Jews and occupies the most
important position in their tradition. The importance of this
term is underlined by the word order in the Greek sentence,
where it occupies an emphatic position at the end of the
sentence. We might translate: '. . . to whom Abraham gave a
tenth of the spoils, yes, the patriarch!'

[5] It is now the aim of the writer to move on to the position of
the levitical priesthood because it embodies the sacrificial
traditions of the Jews. They were given by God the right to
receive tithes and to act as intermediaries, through their
priesthood, between the Israelites and God (see Num.
18.21–24). It is crucial to the argument to show that not only
are they inferior to the new priest, represented by Melchizedek,
but also that they have been superseded.

The fact that the Levites can tithe the people, who are descended from Abraham, would indicate their superiority, but because they themselves are descended from Abraham, and Abraham has been shown to have been inferior to Melchizedek, they too, must be inferior to Melchizedek.

'They are direct descendants . . .' refers here to their brothers.

[6] Since Melchizedek is not descended from Levi, or, for that matter, Abraham, he cannot share their priesthood. But he acted as a priest in regard to Abraham by tithing and blessing him.

[7] Our writer reminds us that Abraham's receiving a blessing demonstrates his inferiority to Melchizedek.

[8] Another mark of Melchizedek's superiority is the testimony from scripture that he is eternal, whereas the Levites are mortal.

9 And one might say that Levi, too, the one who receives tithes, has been tithed through Abraham, 10 for he was still in his father's loins when Melchizedek met him. 11 So if perfection came through the levitical priesthood, since the people have received their laws on the basis of it, what further need was there to set up another priest according to the order of Melchizedek and not name him according to the order of Aaron?

[9–11] The argument goes as follows: since Abraham carried the seed of all his descendants (a common physiological belief in the ancient world), Levi also paid tithes through his father. Furthermore, the levitical priesthood must have been lacking in some way, and at the same time the Mosaic laws, which rest upon the foundation of this priesthood, must also be lacking, because God thought fit to establish another priesthood which was not levitical. Why establish another priest if the levitical priests were sufficient?

[11] What exactly is 'perfection', **teleiôsis**, in this context? Firstly, the capability of performing the task properly, i.e. cleansing the people from sin and bringing them into a full relationship with God. There is also the sense of maturity here: the levitical priesthood was not fully developed; it had not reached, nor could it reach, maturity.

'On the basis of it', **ep'autês**, is an ambiguous phrase. It could also mean 'at the time of it', i.e. at the same time, or 'with a view to it', i.e. in relation to it. Since, however, the Mosaic law was largely concerned with rituals, it is reasonable to say of it that it depended on the establishment of the levitical priesthood.

'The order of Aaron' is another way of referring to the levitical priesthood, because Aaron was descended from Levi.

12 For with the change of priesthood there has to be a change also with the law, 13 since the one about whom these statements are made belongs to another tribe, and none of this tribe has attended at the altar. 14 For it is plain that our Lord is descended from Judah, a tribe in regard to which Moses said nothing about priests. 15 And indeed, it is also even more obvious that another priest like Melchizedek arises, 16 who is born not according to the law of some fleshly commandment but according to the power of life indestructible. 17 For this is the testimony given, 'You are a priest for ever according to the order of Melchizedek'.

[12] Since the Mosaic law is dependent on the levitical priesthood, and inextricably bound up with it, if a new priesthood is established, it must have an effect on the law.

[13, 14] Another difference between the levitical priesthood and the order of Melchizedek is that the new priest, Christ, is from the tribe of Judah, a tribe which was not allowed to serve as priests according to the law of Moses.

We can see, perhaps, from this why two of the Gospel accounts take the trouble to give the genealogy of Jesus. It would appear that the early church was aware of the importance of accounting for the fact that Jesus was not a Levite.

'Altar', **thysiastêrion**, refers to the altar in the Holy of Holies.

[15, 16] What is 'more obvious'? Translations which render **ei** as 'if', rather than 'that', seem to be repeating the previous verse and saying that it is obvious that Jesus is from Judah, if another priest like Melchizedek, i.e. Jesus, is born. To avoid such a repetition the NEB translates vv. 15–16 as follows: '*The argument becomes still clearer, if* the new priest who arises is one like Melchizedek, owing his priesthood not to a system of earth-bound rules but to the power of a life that cannot be destroyed.' 'The argument' has been added in the NEB version, but it is not clear what 'the argument' is.

It is easier to take this verse as saying that it is also more obvious *that* an immortal priest has appeared, not just one who is not of the tribe of Levi. **Ei** can mean 'since', or, as the AV has it, 'for that', but after certain verbs, notably verbs of wondering, **ei** frequently translates as 'that'.

[17] This text from Ps. 110.4 is intended as the proof of the previous verse: i.e. the new priest, Christ, is immortal.

18 For the preceding commandment is set aside due to

its own lack of power or efficacy, 19 since the law
brought nothing to perfection, whereas the introduction of a better hope through which we come close to
God does.

[18, 19] The writer picks up a point raised in v. 11, namely, the
inadequacy of the Mosaic law and priesthood, and the fact that
the new priest was introduced to deal with this problem. The
writer will now develop the argument.

20 And so far as this was not without oath taking,
(for they have been made priests without oath taking
21 while he was made one with oath-taking through
the one who said to him, 'The Lord has sworn, and
will not change his mind, that you will be a priest
for ever'), 22 so much better is the covenant for
which Jesus has become the guarantor. 23 Furthermore, there are more of them made priests, because
they are prevented from continuing as such by death.
24 But he has his priesthood in perpetuity, because
he remains for ever.

[20–22] The importance of the oath is emphasized because the
text from Psalm 110 quoted in v.17 is now recalled with the
addition of the text omitted when it was first quoted, 'The Lord
has sworn, and will not change his mind'. The important
difference between Melchizedek and the levitical priesthood is
that God himself by his oath guaranteed the permanent validity
of the former but, since no oath was involved in the establishment of the latter, or in the ordination of individual priests,
their position was not guaranteed.

'Guarantor', **engyos**, a legal term, one of many in this passage, denoting someone who gives a security or is liable for a sum of money. In other words, because Jesus is the priest of the new covenant, and God has promised that he will last for ever, his covenant has the backing that the old covenant could not have.

[23, 24] There are more priests of the levitical priesthood because they are mortal men and have to be replaced. Christ, on the other hand, because he is immortal, does not need to be replaced. 'In perpetuity', **aparabaton**, literally, 'not capable of being transgressed', hence 'inviolable', 'permanent', or 'perpetual'. Montefiore translates this term as 'which cannot pass to another', but there is no evidence for this usage.

[25] Hence he can also save outright those who approach God through him, since he lives for ever in order to plead for them. 26 For such a high priest was indeed right for us, pure and without evil or stain, separated from sinners and made higher than the heavens, 27 one who does not need like the high priests to offer sacrifice every day, first for his own sins and then for the people's, since he did this once and for all when he offered himself. 28 For the law appoints high priests who are weak, but the wording of the oath which came after the law appoints the Son perfect and for ever.

[25] 'Outright', **eis to panteles**, from the adjective **pantelês**, 'all-accomplishing', an epithet applied in the pagan world to Zeus. Chrysostom observes of this verse, 'See the humiliation, see the manhood . . . he makes intercession continually and whenever needful.'

[26] 'Pure', **hosios**, a word like **hagios**, 'holy', not in the sense of 'sacred', **hieros**, which describes something which it is not permitted for secular or common use, but in the sense of 'blameless'.

'Separated from sinners', **kechôrismenos apo tôn hamartô-lôn**, echoed by the phrase **chôris hamartiâs**, 'free from sin', found in 9.28. This refers not only to the difference between Christ and those for whom he intercedes, but also to the difference between him and the levitical priests.

'Made higher than the heavens', presumably, superior to the angels.

[27] The reference to a daily sacrifice is confusing. Strictly speaking, it was only once a year that the high priest sacrificed, i.e. on the Day of Atonement. So it is not surprising that two later manuscripts amend 'high priests', **archiereis**, to 'priests', **hiereis**. The heads of the twenty-four classes of ordinary priests, however, did sacrifice every day. In fact, they sacrificed a lamb every morning and evening together with an offering of flour and wine. It is likely that our writer is referring to this. There is also evidence for a daily sacrifice by the high priest from Ecclus. 45.14, which in a passage praising Aaron the first high priest says of his sons and descendants (NEB), 'twice every day without fail they present his sacrifice of a whole-offering'.

[28] 'Who are weak', **echontas astheneian**, not only mortal but flawed. This also implies that they are inadequate or powerless, in contrast with the Son who is perfect, i.e. complete, **teteleiômenon**, and capable of performing his priestly function with full power. See the notes on 5.2, 3 and 7.11.

Chapter 8

1 To sum up what I am saying; this is the sort of high priest we have: he sat down at the right hand of the throne of the majesty in the heavens, 2 minister of the Holy Place and of the authentic tabernacle which God set up, not man.

[1, 2] 'To sum up', **kephalaion**, a recapitulation rather than a conclusion. He proceeds with his main argument, which is to show that we can only approach God through Jesus. Melchizedek has become Christ and from now on the writer will be concentrating on his ministry.

'Minister', **leitourgos**, was used in 1.7 to describe the angels serving God. The core meaning of this word is *work for the people*, often with reference to some sacred function. 'Of the Holy Place', literally 'of the holy things', **tôn hagiôn**, from **ta hagia**, rather than, as has been suggested, from **hoi hagioi**, 'the holy people'.

'The authentic tabernacle' is a concept typical of the Platonism prevalent in contemporary Jewish thought. In Wisdom 9.8 Solomon reminds God that he had been told to build the Temple in imitation of the Holy Tabernacle , 'which you prepared beforehand from the beginning'. 'Authentic', **alêthinos**, is a word frequently used by St John and generally translated as 'true'. This slightly distorts the force of the word, since 'authentic' is closer to 'real' than to 'true'.

It might be helpful, since our writer has paused for a summary, to list the differences between Melchizedek/Christ and the levitical high priest.

According to the order of Melchizedek	*According to the order of Aaron*
Superior to Abraham because 1. he blesses him	Abraham 1. is blessed by Melchizedek
2. he receives tithes from him and so from all his descendants	2. gives him tithes and since he carries Levi 'in his loins', Levi is in the same relationship
He is immortal, for ever and permanent	He is mortal, repeated and temporary
One	Many
Established by God's oath	No oath
Sinless – does not need to sacrifice	Sinner – must also sacrifice for himself
Sacrifices himself	Sacrifices animals
Efficacious and powerful	Ineffective and feeble
Sacrifice was once and for all	Sacrifice is daily
Ministers in the Heavenly Tabernacle	Ministers in the Temple on earth
Tribe of Judah (Christ)	Tribe of Levi

3 For every high priest is appointed to offer gifts and sacrifices; hence he also has to have something to offer. 4 However, if he were on earth he would not be a

priest, since there are those who offer gifts according to the law, 5 who serve with a picture and a shadow of the heavenly place, as Moses was ordered to do when he was about to finish the tabernacle. For he says, 'See that you do everything according to the pattern shown you on the mountain'.

[3] There is no need to follow Montefiore's suggestion that the last part of this verse has to be translated as though it refers to a past action – 'hence it was necessary for him too to have had something to offer'. His reason for this is because he objects to the idea that Jesus continually offers his blood in heaven. He says, 'Jesus' present ministry in heaven is intercession, not offering; and so it was in the past that he had to have had something to offer.'

Apart from the fact that 'blood' is not mentioned here, it seems unnecessary to claim that the sacrifice on Calvary, because it occurred in historical time and was therefore over and done with, cannot be seen as occurring in eternity. Most Christians of the first century would have been familiar with the concept that Jesus is offering himself as an eternal sacrifice in heaven. Rev. 5.6 presents us with a vision of the 'lamb standing as though slaughtered', **arnion hestêkos hôs es-phagmenon,** a paradoxical representation of the fact that Christ is in heaven both as living and sacrificed at the same time.

As to Montefiore's suggestion that Jesus' ministry is intercession, not offering, our writer, having said earlier that Christ is the minister of the Holy Place in heaven, says in this verse that he is offering something, and it would appear from the comparison with the earthly high priests who offer 'gifts and sacrifices', that Christ's offering cannot be the prayers and intercessions mentioned in 7.25.

[4] 'However', **oun**, is the best reading, but some later manuscripts give **gar**, 'for', which is the one adopted by the AV.

The reasoning is that Christ could not be a priest on earth as he is of the tribe of Judah, but as he is a priest in heaven, this priesthood has superseded the one on earth.

[5] 'With a picture', **hypodeigmati**, or 'by example'. It is a characteristic of Platonism to believe that everything on earth is a mere copy or shadow of an ideal which is invisible to ordinary human beings. The quotation is from Ex. 25.40.

6 But now he has gained a ministry so much the superior as the covenant of which he is the mediator is the better, and one which is ordained on better promises. 7 For if the first one had been blameless, there would have been no search for a place for the second.

[6] A complicated sentence, which simply interpreted means, 'Christ's ministry is better because the covenant on which it is based is better'.

'Better promises', because they really do save from sin and death and they give direct access to God. The use of the term 'mediator' here is interesting. Unlike the priest of the old covenant, who stands between us and God, this new mediator, through whom the new covenant was made, brings us into God's presence.

[7] 'The first (one)', refers either to 'ministry', **leitourgiâ**, or to 'covenant', **diathêkê**.

The argument is that God would not have made the first covenant obsolete if it had been effective and adequate.

8 For it is by way of blaming them that he says, 'Behold the days are coming,' says the Lord, 'when I shall complete a new covenant with the house of Israel and with the house of Judah, 9 not according to the covenant which I made with their fathers on the day when I took them by the hand to lead them out of the land of Egypt, because they did not abide by my covenant and I ignored them,' says the Lord. 10 'For this is the covenant which I shall make with the house of Israel after those days;' says the Lord, 'in giving my laws, I will write them in their mind and on their hearts, and I shall be a God to them and they will be a people to me, 11 and each will not teach his fellow citizen or each his brother saying, "Know the Lord", because everyone of them shall know me, from the small to the great, 12 since I will be merciful to their unrighteousness and I will no longer remember their sins.' 13 By saying 'new', he has made the first obsolete, and that which is made obsolete and old comes close to being abolished.

[8–12] This passage is from Jer. 31.31–34, and again seems to be from memory, as there are minor variations in vocabulary and phrasing throughout. This text supports the previous argument: 1. there was a need to abolish the old covenant, as it was ineffective, and 2. the new covenant gives the people direct access to God.

[13] 'Obsolete' is literally 'antiquated', from the Greek verb **palaiöô**, 'to make old'.

'Comes close to being abolished', **engys aphanismou**, literally, '(is) near to disappearing'. Why does he not say simply that it was abolished? Probably because he regards the old covenant as continuing after Jeremiah's prophecy. It was actually abolished when Christ's sacrifice took place and the new high priest entered heaven.

Chapter 9

1 The first [covenant], indeed, had rules for service and the Holy Place in the world. 2 For the first tabernacle was prepared with the candlestick, the table and the display of loaves, which is called the Holy Place, 3 and behind the second veil was the tabernacle called the Holy of Holies, 4 with a golden censer and the Ark of the Covenant covered all over with gold, and inside it was the golden jar holding the manna, the rod of Aaron which sprouted, and the tablets of the covenant. 5 Over it are the Cherubim of Glory overshadowing the Mercy Seat. Of these we cannot speak now in detail. 6 Since these are the arrangements that have been made, the priests enter the first tabernacle all the time when they are performing their services, 7 but only the high priest goes into the second tabernacle once a year, and that not without making a blood-offering for himself and the mistakes of the people.

[1–7] The description of the tabernacle here is based on that given in Exodus 25–26, and refers to the original tent in the wilderness. There are minor discrepancies. For example, there was originally only one tent divided into two areas by the veil, while our writer speaks of two tents, Vulg. *tabernacula*. These discrepancies reflect the changes made during the Temple's history. The original single candlestick became ten when the Tent was superseded by the Temple, and other changes occurred with the passage of time.

Commentators have been particularly struck by the fact that the censer, **thûmiâtêrion**, is described as being in the inner shrine, when traditionally it was outside. The jar containing the manna and Aaron's rod were also absent. Various explanations are given. For instance, the term **thûmiâtêrion** could be shorthand for **thysiastêrion tou thûmiâmatos**, 'the altar of incense', and although Ex. 30.6 seems to imply that it was not in the inner shrine, Ex. 40.5 speaks of the altar for the incense as being in front of the ark. According to Lev. 16.12–13 the censer was definitely taken into the inner shrine on the Day of Atonement, and our writer is probably thinking of the arrangements made on that occasion. Perhaps by the first century AD the censer was normally situated in the Holy of Holies. For the writer's purpose archaeological exactitude is not important. He was doubtless aware of the various changes that had taken place in the arrangement of the Temple, but his main theme is the contrast between the old and the new.

[1] No noun is given in the text after 'first', but the writer is clearly referring to the subject of the previous verse, i.e. the covenant. 'Rules for service', **dikaiômata latreiâs**, are literally 'ordinances of worship'.

'The Holy Place in the world', **to hagion kosmikon**, or, as the Vulgate has it, *sanctum saeculare*, is the earthly equivalent of the heavenly Temple.

[2] 'Which is called the Holy Place', **hêtis legetai hagia**. Montefiore takes **hagia** as feminine singular, **hagiâ**, rather than neuter plural, and as describing the tabernacle, **skênê**. He translates this clause as 'this tent is called Holy'. However, we

know from other references to the tabernacle that in this context the word is always treated as a neuter plural, **(ta) hagia**, 'the Holy Things'. The omission of the article **ta**, 'the', is not significant. Several manuscripts restore it, but omission of the article is common in Greek of this period. The same grammatical usage can be observed in v. 3, where the tabernacle is called **hagia hagiôn**, and both articles have been omitted.

[5] 'Of these we cannot now speak in detail' should not be interpreted as though the writer felt the subject was too sacred; rather, it would take too much time and was not relevant to his theme.

[7] 'Mistakes' here refers to sins of omission or involuntary lapses, **agnoêmata**, literally, 'ignorances'. It is appropriate here where the writer is contrasting the repeated ritual cleansing of petty sins with the powerful act of the new high priest who has freed human beings once and for all from engrained sin.

8 So the Holy Spirit shows that the way into the Holy Place is not yet revealed while the first tabernacle has a place; 9 and this is an allegory applying to the present time, in which gifts and sacrifices are offered which cannot make the worshipper perfect in regard to his conscience, 10 since they are only fleshly ordinances, which were imposed until the time of reformation in regard to food, drink and various purifications.

[8–10] This passage, at first sight, is not easy to follow. One reason for this is that the reference in v. 8 to the 'first' tabernacle is ambiguous: is it the original tabernacle of Moses, or, for that matter, the Solomonian or the Herodian Temple?

Or is the 'first' tabernacle simply the Holy Place, i.e. the first part of the shrine?

The clue to interpretation is given in v. 9 – 'This is an allegory'. The writer said in v. 6 that all the priests go into the first part of the shrine daily and now adds that no proper atonement takes place ('which cannot make . . . perfect . . .'), but when the single high priest goes into the Holy of Holies, and that only once a year, as he stated in v. 7, a blood sacrifice takes place which does atone for sin. He interprets this as a symbol of the new dispensation whereby the Judaic ritual, which cannot properly atone for sin, is represented by the first part of the shrine, i.e. the Holy Place, and the heavenly tabernacle with its one high priest Jesus Christ is represented by the old Holy of Holies, which was entered once a year by the one levitical high priest.

Chrysostom clearly takes the passage in this sense from the start of chapter 9. His comment on v. 1 is, 'The Holy Place is a symbol (**typos**) of the former period, for there all things are done by sacrifices, but the Holy of Holies (is a symbol) of this that is now present.'

[8] 'The Holy Spirit', speaking, that is, through Scripture.

'Has a place', **echousês stasin**. Is the writer implying that the first tabernacle physically no longer exists? In other words, is he speaking after the destruction of the Temple in 70? No, he is simply noting that the ritual (and law) of Moses was valid until the time when the new covenant began to operate. After that there is no place for it. The verb he uses has an exact meaning: **echein stasin** is not 'to exist', but rather 'to have a position', that is, 'to have a function'.

[9] This verse may answer the question raised in the previous one regarding the existence of the Temple at the time the writer

is speaking. It would appear that gifts and sacrifices were still being offered at the time of his writing.

[10] 'The time of reformation' is the new era ushered in by Christ's sacrifice on the cross. It is not possible to take this phrase as referring to his second coming, since it would necessarily follow from that interpretation that the 'fleshly ordinances' remain valid until that time.

11 But Christ has appeared as a high priest of the good things that have come about through the greater and more perfect tabernacle, one not made by hands, that is, not of this creation, 12 and has entered the Holy Place once and for all, not through the blood of goats or calves, but through his own blood, having obtained an everlasting ransom. 13 For if the blood of goats and bulls and the ash of a heifer sprinkled on the defiled sanctifies them in regard to fleshly purity, 14 how much more will the blood of Christ, who through the Eternal Spirit offered himself blameless to God, cleanse our conscience from dead works to worship the living God?

[11] This verse has provoked much comment. Firstly we have a variant reading, **mellontôn**, 'that are to come', found in some good manuscripts. The better reading, however, appears to be **genomenôn**, 'that have come about', preferred by Chrysostom and Origen. It would be odd to speak of Christ as a high priest of a covenant not yet in operation, when it is clear throughout this letter that the writer regards the covenant as already operative. In other words, the 'good things' have already happened.

Next we have two questions: 1. did Christ 'appear' through the tabernacle, or did the good things come about through the tabernacle? 2. Does the 'tabernacle' have another meaning?

Firstly, it would be strange to say that Christ appeared through one tabernacle and entered another. Both tabernacles would have to be heavenly ones, the first being 'not made by hands', and 'not of this creation', and the second presumably the heavenly temple. It does not make it easier if we take **dia**, 'through', as meaning 'by means of'. The difficulty remains. On the other hand, it makes perfect sense to say that the 'good things', i.e. the benefits of the new covenant, have come to us through the operation of the heavenly tabernacle where Christ is the high priest of God the Father. God's grace acting in heaven has enabled his Son to cleanse his people from sin.

As to the second question, some have suggested that the 'tabernacle' is Christ's body, but although we might accept that it was 'not made by hands', it certainly was 'of this creation', i.e. a real and material body. Mark 14.58 speaks of the high priests accusing Christ of boasting that he would destroy 'this temple made by hands and in three days build another *not made by hands*'. Although that can be taken as a reference to his resurrected body, such an interpretation is not relevant here.

[12] 'The Holy Place', **ta hagia,** is the heavenly Temple. Strictly speaking we would have expected 'the Holy of Holies', **hagia hagiôn**. Indeed this reading has been found in a late manuscript, but our writer uses the expression loosely.

'Through his own blood, having obtained an everlasting ransom', is reminiscent of Titus 2.14, 'who gave himself for us, to ransom us from every sin'.

[13] 'The defiled', **tous kekoinômenous**, a specific term relating to ritual defilement, literally, 'made common', not the

sinful state which is cleansed by the saving power of Christ's sacrifice. The old rites only 'sanctified' in a limited sense. For example, contact with a dead body necessitated a ritual of cleansing. Such pollution was often accidental and certainly not what we would regard as a sin, even if deliberate. See the note on v. 7.

For an account of the ritual referred to, see Numbers 19 *passim*.

[14] 'Eternal', **aiôniou**, has been emended to 'holy', **hagiou**, in some manuscripts. Both Chrysostom and Jerome (Vulg. *sanctum*) assume **hagiou** to be the correct reading. There is, however, no reason why the Spirit of God should not be given this epithet. We do not need to exclude the Holy Spirit from the redemptive process through which we inherit eternal life by Christ's sacrifice. We are reminded of the Pauline view of the old covenant which has to do with **sarx**, 'flesh', and the new which operates through **pneuma**, 'spirit'. Christ's self-sacrifice took place not as part of a fleshly rite but by the operation of the Spirit.

Montefiore takes the expression 'eternal spirit' as 'eternal nature', and thinks it refers to 'the power of a life that nothing can destroy' (his version of the phrase 'the power of life indestructible' in 7.16). He rejects the idea that here it means 'the Holy Spirit' and comments that 'self-sacrifice was offered by Christ in his eternal nature'. It is, however, impossible to translate **pneuma** as 'nature', even if we accept his comment.

'Dead works', as in 6.1, are sins. The contrast between 'dead' works and the 'living' God is underlined in the Greek word order.

15 And for this reason, he is the mediator of a new testament, since his death occurs for the redemption of

trespasses which were the consequence of the first testament, so that those who are called may receive the promise of their eternal inheritance. 16 For where you have a testament, the death of the one who makes it has to occur, 17 since a testament is valid after death and never comes into force while the testator is alive. 18 Hence even the first testament was not inaugurated without blood.

[15–18] The difficulty of this passage is due to the fact that **diathêkê**, which we have translated so far as 'covenant', also means 'will', i.e. 'testament', *testamentum*. As a will does not come into force before the person making the will has died, so Christ's death is necessary before the new **diathêkê** can come into effect.

[15] 'Mediator', **mesîtês**, is also used to describe Moses who mediated the first covenant between man and God.

The statement that the trespasses occurred as a consequence of the first covenant is put more starkly by Paul in Rom. 7.8–10, 'For without the law sin was dead. I lived without the law once, but when the commandment came, sin revived and I died.' Paul, of course, develops this theme fully in Romans. Our writer would appear to be treating Paul's argument as already familiar to his audience. There is no need to avoid describing sin as the *consequence* of the covenant which established the Law. Paul makes it quite explicit that sin came into force *because of* the Law, not simply as the next stage in the historical process or a phenomenon which happened to occur along with the operation of the Law.

[16] Because we have to translate **diathêkê** in two different ways, we lose in English the force and subtlety of the Greek.

Our writer knew quite well that covenants and testaments are not the same, but he sees an opportunity to extract a prophetic meaning from the use of the term.

'To occur', **pheresthai**, which could also be translated 'to be endured', and, according to Moffatt, 'to be announced'.

[18] Our writer now reverts to the first covenant/testament of Moses and argues that, as blood was shed on that occasion, the first covenant involved death also. Thus both covenants are also testaments.

'Was inaugurated', **engkekainistai**, Vulg. *dedicatum est*, literally, 'was renewed'. The root of this verb is **kainos**, 'new', which is found also in the Encaenia or 'Feast of Re-dedication' which marks the restoration of the Temple in Jerusalem in 165 BC by the Maccabees. Here the meaning is not 'was restored', since there had been no covenant beforehand, but rather 'was newly established'.

19 For after speaking to all the people about every commandment according to the law, Moses took the blood of calves and goats with water, red wool and hyssop, and sprinkled both the book itself and all the people 20 saying, 'This is the blood of the testament which God has imposed on you', 21 and he sprinkled the tabernacle and all the vessels of the service likewise with blood. 22 Indeed nearly all things are purified by blood according to the law, and no pardon is effected without the shedding of blood.

[19] The account given in Ex. 24.3–8 differs in several details from that given here. In the original ritual no goats are sacrificed, nor is there any mention of water, red wool or

hyssop. Furthermore, Moses sprinkles the altar, not the book. It is possible that our writer is giving a general list of various rituals enjoined by the Mosaic code culled from other references, such as Lev. 14. 4–7 and Num. 19.6–19, and indeed rituals that were characteristic of later Judaic rites. The evidence for this is his reference to 'speaking to all the people *about every commandment* according to the law'. 'Hyssop', incidentally, according to Montefiore, is probably marjoram.

[20] This quotation from Ex. 24.8 has been slightly but significantly altered to remind his audience of the words of Christ at the institution of the Last Supper. Whereas the Exodus account says 'Behold . . .', **idou** in the Septuagint version, all three Gospel accounts give 'This . . .', **touto**. Chrysostom has no doubt that the reference is deliberate and says, 'With this blood not Moses but Christ sprinkled us, through the word which was spoken: "This is the blood of the new testament, for the remission of sins." '

There is no need to argue, as some commentators do, that our writer is not concerned in this letter with the eucharist. He is writing at a time when the Roman authorities were very disturbed by the persistent rumours of cannibalism practised by Christians. This was clearly one of the accusations pursued by Pliny when he was interrogating Christians in Bithynia (see Book 10, letter 96, where one might sense his disappointment when he discovers that the food that was eaten was normal!). Consequently our writer is necessarily reticent about the eucharist. His audience, however, would have seen the connection. The pagan obsession with cannibalism at the eucharist continued throughout the next century and is noted by contemporary Christian writers.

[22] 'Nearly all things are purified by blood' is taken by Chrysostom as an admission that the purification of the old

covenant was half-complete and not a perfect remission. The general view, however, is that it means simply that blood was not always used in purification rituals. Chrysostom may very well be right, as our writer goes on to say that 'no pardon is effected without the shedding of blood', which implies that effective, not just symbolic, purification involves blood-shedding.

23 So the copies of the heavenly things have to be purified by these, but the heavenly things themselves by sacrifices which are better than them. 24 For Christ has not entered a sanctuary made by hands, a copy of the real place, but heaven itself, to appear now before the face of God on our behalf, 25 but not to make frequent offerings of himself, like the high priest who enters the sanctuary every year with the blood of another, 26 since he would have had to suffer many times since the foundation of the world; but now he has appeared once and for all at the end of time for the remission of sins through his own sacrifice. 27 And inasmuch as human beings have to face death once and after that the judgment, 28 so Christ also was offered up once to take away the sins of many and he will be seen a second time without sin by those who eagerly look to him for their salvation.

[23–28] The writer now turns from the sacrifice of the Mosaic covenant to the sacrifice of Christ and contrasts the repetition of the old rituals with the singularity of his self-offering.

[23] It appears as though the writer is saying that the heavenly temple had to be purified, but this is not his intention. His use

of antithesis can obscure his argument. The point he is making is that it is only in heaven that a real purification can take place. Chrysostom relates the worship of the church on earth to that in heaven and says of 'the heavenly things', **ta epourania**, that they are 'ours', **ta hêmetera**. 'It follows then that our things are in heaven, and heavenly things are ours, even though they be accomplished on earth.'

[24–25] Although Christ does not repeat his self-sacrifice, he presents his sacrifice to God in person and intercedes 'now', **nûn**, that is, eternally, for us.

[26] The argument is a *reductio ad absurdum*; Christ, like any human being, cannot die more than once. Therefore, if, like the high priest, he had to repeat his sacrifice, he would have had to be killed several times, which is clearly impossible.

'Remission', **athetêsis**, literally, 'a setting aside'.

'At the end of time', **epi synteleiâi tôn aiônôn**, literally, 'at the completion of the ages', reminds us of I Peter 1.20 which, in speaking of Christ's sacrifice, says of him that he was 'foreordained *before the foundation of the world*, **pro katabolês kosmou** ('since the foundation of the world' in this verse of Hebrews is **apo katabolês kosmou**), but revealed '*at the end of the times*, **ep'eschatou tôn chronôn**, because of you'. The correspondence is striking.

[28] 'Without sin', **chôris hamartiâs**, has its parallel in 7.26, **kechôrismenos apo tôn hamartôlôn**, 'separated from sinners', or, in other words, 'sinless'. Montefiore, however, translates this phrase as 'not to deal with sin', introducing the interesting notion that at the Last Judgment Christ's second advent 'will have no reference to sin at all, since he dealt with that at his first advent'. It is, however, more likely that this reference to

Christ's sinlessness is because our writer is contrasting him here with the earthly high priest who offers sacrifice for his own sins as well as for those of the people.

Chapter 10

1 For the law holds a shadow of the good things to come, not the actual form of reality, and with the same sacrifices which they offer every year, it can never make perfect for all time those who attend. 2 After all, would they not have stopped making their offerings, because the worshippers having been purified once and for all would no longer have any sense of guilt? 3 But in fact, in these [sacrifices] there is a commemoration of sin every year. 4 For it is impossible for the blood of bulls and goats to take away sins.

[1] 'Of the good things to come', **tôn mellontôn agathôn**, could refer to either the bliss of the world to come or the new covenant which is already in operation now, but was in the future at the time the old covenant was established.

'The actual form of reality', **autên tên eikona tôn pragmatôn**, literally, 'the very image of things', is not an easy phrase to understand, and this has probably been the reason why the manuscripts have variant readings of this passage. The key word **eikôn**, translated here as 'form', requires some explanation. The root meaning of the word is 'likeness', and we can use it to express two different ideas. On the one hand, *x* can be like *y*, but, *because* it is like, it is not the same as *y*; on the other hand, *x* can be like *y* because it *is* the same as *y*. We can see the two concepts coming together in Col. 1.15, where Paul refers to Christ, 'who is the **eikôn** of the invisible God'. Our writer is using the term in its Platonic sense as a synonym for 'idea' or 'form'. See Plato's *Cratylus* 306 E, where we have **eikonas tôn pragmatôn**, 'the Forms of material things'. Chrysostom saw that this was the sense intended and takes **eikôn** here as a synonym for **alêtheia**, 'truth', or 'reality'.

'For all time', **eis to diênekes**, qualifies 'make perfect', not 'who attend'. In other words, it does not mean 'continually'. See note on 7.3.

[2] To paraphrase this verse: the fact that the priests of the old dispensation need to repeat their sacrifices every year shows that they are ineffectual, because if they actually did take away sin, there would be no need to repeat them.

[3,4] 'Commemoration', **anamnêsis**, is the word used at the institution of the Lord's Supper, 'Do this *in remembrance of me*', **eis tên emên anamnêsin**, Luke 22.19. Our writer is saying in effect that the yearly sacrifice serves to remind the people, and God, of their sins, as the blood of animals is incapable of wiping out sin.

5 Therefore, when he comes into the world, he says, 'You did not want a sacrifice and an offering, but you prepared a body for me; 6 you did not appreciate burnt offerings and sin-offerings. 7 Then I said, "Behold I have come, (in the roll of the book it is written about me), to do your will, O God".' 8 When he says above, 'You did not want or appreciate sacrifices, offerings, burnt offerings and sin-offerings' (things that are offered according to the law), 9 then he has said,

'Behold, I have come to do your will'. He abolishes the first in order to establish the second, 10 and we have been sanctified by this will through the offering of the body of Jesus Christ once and for all.

[5] The writer visualizes Christ saying these words (from Ps. 40.6–8) at his incarnation. The Hebrew version has 'ears', rather than 'body', **sôma** (in the AV, 'mine ears hast thou opened'), which gives a different sense, i.e. obeying God is better than ritual sacrifice. Our writer is using the Septuagint version, which allows him to take the quotation in a Messianic sense, although this version can be interpreted in a similar way to the Hebrew, i.e. my body was given to me to serve you.

[6] There is a minor variation here, **eudokêsas,** 'you appreciated', rather than the Septuagint **ezêtêsas,** 'you sought'; proof again that the writer is quoting from memory.

[7] In the original Psalm, 'the roll of the book' is probably the law of Moses which was prescribed for the speaker (the Hebrew reads, 'for me', not 'about me'). It is unlikely that our writer is thinking of passages of scripture which speak of the necessity to obey God, since he is concerned with prophecies of the coming of the Messiah.

[8] It is interesting to note that, in referring to his previous quotation, our writer does not repeat it exactly, but changes singulars to plurals and alters the word order.

[9] 'The first' = the old sacrifices ; 'the second' = the sacrifice of the incarnate Christ.

[10] 'Sanctified', literally, 'having been made holy', **hêgiasmenoi,** not simply 'justified'. In other words, the sacrifice of

Christ has not just cleared the slate and wiped out the debts of sin; it has actually made us 'holy', **hagioi**.

'This will' is both God's original plan and Christ's willingness to accept his Father's decision.

11 And every priest stands day by day ministering and offering many times the same sacrifices which can never take away sins. 12 But this one, after offering a single sacrifice for sins for ever, sat down at the right hand of God, 13 awaiting the future when his enemies are set as a footstool beneath his feet. 14 For by a single offering he has made those being sanctified perfect for ever.

[11] The 'priest', or 'high priest' according to some manuscripts, is standing in contrast to the seated Christ of the next verse.

'Take away', **perielein,** is literally 'to strip off', like a skin.

[12] 'After offering', **prosenengkâs,** aorist participle of **prospherô**. The Vulgate translates with a present participle, *offerens*, but we need not extract any theological significance from this, as it is not unusual in late Latin to use present participles as we do in English, i.e. without a strict temporal meaning.

'For ever' can be taken with the clause or with the main verb 'sat down'. The significance of Christ sitting at the right hand of God is that he is not a worshipper or inferior to God, but one who shares his position. In Rev. 5.6 the Lamb is depicted as 'in the midst of the throne'.

[13] Who are his 'enemies'? Some commentators shrink from this question, presumably because they feel it is merely a

metaphor. Chrysostom does not hesitate to answer the question; they are 'all unbelievers: the demons'.

[14] The present participle, **hagiazomenous**, 'being sanctified', is in contrast with the perfect participle, **hēgiasmenoi,** of v. 10, and seems to contradict it. But the writer is saying something of great depth; paradoxically, the believer has been 'perfected' (see the notes on the use of this verb in 2.10 and 5.9), because Christ's self-sacrifice is sufficient, and there is nothing lacking for salvation. We remember Christ's last word on the cross, 'It is finished', **tetelestai**, John 19.30. On the other hand, 'holiness' is a dynamic process; the 'holy' must become more 'holy'. We have been sanctified, as v. 10 says, by the sacrifice of Christ, but we have further to go.

15 And the Holy Spirit also bears witness to us. For, after saying, 16 'This is the covenant that I shall make with them after those days (says the Lord), in giving my laws I shall write them on their hearts and on their mind, 17 and I will remember no more their sins and transgressions.' 18 And where there is a forgiveness of these, there is no longer an offering for sin.

[15–18] To summarize his argument, the writer refers back to the passage of Jeremiah he quoted at length in 8.8–12, repeating 10 and 12 with variations and omissions.

[15] 'The Holy Spirit', as in 9.8, speaking through scripture.

[18] In other words, because God says he will no longer remember their sins, there is no need to offer sacrifices for those sins.

19 So, then, brothers and sisters, having the freedom to enter the sanctuary by the blood of Jesus, 20 by a fresh and living road, which he has inaugurated for us through the veil, that is, his flesh, 21 and having a great high priest over the house of God, 22 let us approach with a true heart in complete trust with hearts purified from an evil conscience, and our bodies washed with pure water.

[19] For 'freedom', **parrhêsiân,** see the note on 3.6.

[20] There are two powerful and complex metaphors in this verse which need to be examined. Firstly, what is this 'fresh and living road'? The key is found in the word translated as 'fresh', **prosphaton.** This is 'fresh' in the sense of 'not decomposed', the opposite of 'stale', and, coupled with 'living', is a perfect description of clean running water. It does not mean 'new' in the sense of 'novel'. This would appear to be a reference to the water of baptism through which the believer is cleansed from sin and admitted to fellowship with Christ. The allusion is picked up again in v. 22. Chrysostom seems to identify the 'living way' with **ta prostagmata,** that is, the Christian ordinances, which may include other rites besides baptism.

Next we turn to 'the veil'. The writer identifies 'the veil' with 'his flesh', adding 'that is', **tout' estin,** to underline the identification. It appears at first sight strange to say that we have to enter through Christ's flesh, but we can understand this as meaning that we have to die with Christ, that is, share the death of his body, in order to be raised into everlasting life. Hence, the way into the Holy of Holies is through the new veil of Christ's flesh.

Paul speaks in Col. 2.12 of our being buried with Christ in baptism, and again in Rom. 6.4 says, 'we were buried with him through baptism into death'. Such passages clearly support the identification of the 'fresh and living way' with baptism. The Romans passage can be seen almost as the prose equivalent of our poetical verse 20.

There is support for the identification of the veil with Christ's body in Mark 15.37–38, 'And Jesus uttering a loud cry, breathed his last, and the veil of the temple was split in two from top to bottom'. The tearing of the veil can be taken as emblematic of the tearing of Christ's flesh on the cross. Chrysostom, while accepting the identification of the veil with Christ's flesh, explores the metaphor further and adds, 'and with good reason did he call [the flesh] "a veil". For when it was lifted up on high, then the things in heaven appeared.'

Objections to this interpretation have been raised, principally on the grounds that the veil is not used in the rest of this letter in this sense, but denotes only the barrier that exists between God and man. It has been suggested that 'a fresh and living way' refers to 'his flesh'. In other words, we enter through the veil into the presence of God via the sacrifice of Christ's body.

[22] 'True', **alêthinês**, i.e. 'sincere', 'genuine'. The repetition of 'heart(s)' is odd but there is no justification for altering what is only stylistically suspect.

'Our bodies washed with pure water' is a clear reference to baptism, and it is interesting to see an echo of the 'fresh and living' of v. 20 in the adjective 'pure', **katharôi**. Note that this outward ceremony has its inward spiritual counterpart in 'with hearts purified from an evil conscience'. 'Purified', literally, 'sprinkled', **rherantismenoi**, reminds one of the Mosaic counterpart, the sprinkling of the polluted with the ashes of the red heifer mentioned in 9.13. The same verb, **rhantizô**, is used there. Our writer does not mention the fact that the ashes had to be mixed with running, i.e. living, water, (see Num. 19.17–19). This makes the parallel with baptism even more striking.

23 Let us keep steadfast the confession of hope, for he who promised is trustworthy; 24 and let us watch out for one another, to the encouragement of love and good works, 25 not neglecting to meet together, as some are accustomed to do, but giving encouragement, and that all the more so as you see the day approaching. 26 For if we willingly sin after receiving the knowledge of the truth, there is no longer left any sacrifice for sins, 27 but a terrified expectation of judgment and a fiery indignation which will devour the hostile. 28 Anyone who rejected the law of Moses was put to death without mercy on the testimony of two or three witnesses. 29 How much worse will be the punishment he shall be judged worthy of, who has trampled on the son of God, profaned the blood of the covenant, by which he was sanctified, and insulted the Spirit of grace? 30 For we know him who said, 'Vengeance is mine; I will repay', and again, 'The Lord shall judge his people'. 31 It is a frightening thing to fall into the hands of the living God.

[23–31] Our writer's audience are warned again of the consequences of apostasy, and at the same time encouraged to remain faithful and regular attenders at meetings of the church. This passage echoes closely the sentiments of 6.1–12, but he skilfully avoids repeating himself.

[23] 'Confession', **homologiân**; see the note on 3.1.

[24] 'Let us watch out for', **katanöômen**, or 'observe', 'keep an eye on'. Note the association of love and good works, already seen in 6.10. As Paul argues in II Cor. 8.8–24, the proof of love is shown by the performance of good deeds.

[25] This verse is reminiscent of II Thess. 2.1–2, not only in its use of the rare word **episynagôgê**, 'gathering together', but also in its reference to the second coming of Christ. This word, however, is used in a different sense, as the context of the Thessalonians passage makes clear: '. . . in the matter of the coming (**parousiâs**) of our Lord Jesus Christ and our gathering to him (**hêmôn episynagôgês ep' auton**) . . .' Obviously Paul is thinking of the in-gathering of the faithful to Christ on the last day, whereas our writer means by this word a meeting for worship.

[26] Chrysostom points out that this verse does not take away the possibility of repentance or forgiveness, but that, 'there is no more a second cross'. In other words, Christ's sacrifice cannot be repeated. Since the word 'willingly', **hekousiôs** (which can also be translated as 'wilfully'), is in an emphatic position in the sentence, Chrysostom draws attention to the word, making it clear that there *is* pardon for those who are not wilful, i.e. deliberate, sinners.

[27] 'Fiery indignation', **pyros zêlos**, is a reference to Zeph. 1.18, 'but the whole land shall be devoured *by the fire of his jealousy*' (AV). This phrase is close to the Sept. reading, **en pyri zêlou**. Our writer has omitted the first part of the verse which says, 'Neither their silver nor their gold shall be able to deliver them in the day of the Lord's wrath', but his audience would have known the reference to the day of the Lord of which v. 25 had reminded them. It is interesting that Chrysostom, in his homily on this passage, goes on to accuse of idolatry women

who keep clothes made of gold thread safe in their wardrobes and never wear them.

[28] The reference is to Deut. 17.6 and is a punishment laid down for those who have worshipped other gods.

[29] This verse is interpreted both by Chrysostom and Montefiore as a condemnation of those who have shared in the eucharist unworthily or have absented themselves without good cause. It is, however, possible to see it as a reference to the apostates who have escaped punishment from the Roman authorities by performing an act which was a public insult or repudiation of Christ. Pliny makes it plain that such acts would procure an acquittal; see the note on 6.6.

'By which he was sanctified', **en hôi hêgiasthê**, is omitted in one manuscript but is a firm reading. See above vv. 10 and 14.

'The Spirit of grace', i.e. the Holy Spirit. See the note on 'Eternal Spirit', 9.14.

[30] The quotation, from Deut. 32.35, 'To me belongeth vengeance, and recompence' (AV), which Paul also uses in Romans 12.19, is not from the Sept. we know. It has been suggested that it comes from a Targum, an Aramaic translation of the OT, but it could be an alternative reading current at the time. The second quotation is from Deut. 32–36.

32 But remember the old days, when, after seeing the light, you endured a great trial of suffering, 33 sometimes exhibited with insults and oppression, and sometimes fellow-partners of those treated in this way. 34 For, indeed, you felt for prisoners, and took the plundering of your goods with joy, knowing that you have a better and enduring property. 35 Do not throw

away your right of access, which brings a great recompense. 36 For you need patience to win your promise after doing the will of God. 37 'Just a little while longer', and, 'he who is coming will arrive and will not tarry'; 38 'The just person shall live by faith in me', and, 'if he draws back, my soul does not rejoice in him'. 39 But we are not the kind who draw back to our destruction, but those who have faith for the gaining of life.

[32] For 'after seeing the light' see the note on 6.4.

This verse refers to a previous period of persecution, but there is insufficient evidence for us to put this into a particular historical setting. Chrysostom relates the trouble to a time when the new converts were being persecuted by their own people. This would have involved the Roman authorities, who, in dealing with the tension, would have made little distinction between rival factions of those they saw simply as trouble-makers.

[33] 'Exhibited', **theatrizomenoi**, literally, 'put on the stage'. It is not necessary to assume that this meant that they actually appeared on the stage in some degrading performance, though one need not rule this out, but rather that they had to appear in public, perhaps at a judicial tribunal. Chrysostom thinks this refers to the treatment of the apostles themselves.

'Fellow-partners', not just 'associates', but 'sharers', **koinônoi**, providing a share of their own resources. It is unfortunate that nowadays the word 'share' tends to refer only to verbal communication. See note on 2.14.

[34] Some later manuscripts add 'in heaven' to the sentence, in

case the reader should be wondering where the 'better and-enduring property' might be located.

[35] 'Right of access', **parrhêsiân**; see note on 3.6.

'The recompense' is not just the comfort of knowing they had access but an actual reward awaiting them in heaven. Modern neurosis about altruism has no place here.

[36] 'Win your promise', see note on previous verse.

[37–38] This passage is a mosaic of quotations from Isa. 26.20, 'just a little while longer', and Hab. 2.3–4, the latter slightly amended and with v. 4 in reverse order. There are variations in the text; for example, 'in me' (literally, 'of me', **mou**) is omitted by some, probably to conform with Rom. 1.17. Also the same word has been taken by others with 'the just' rather than 'by faith', producing the translation, 'my righteous one shall live by faith'. The AV renders the latter part of Hab. 2.4 as 'the just shall live by his faith'.

[39] 'For the gaining of life', **eis peripoiêsin psûchês. Peripoiêsis** is a term meaning either 'acquisition' or 'preservation'. **Psûchê** is often translated as 'soul' but is really the breath of life', and is used here to denote 'eternal life'.

Chapter 11

1 Faith is the foundation of our hopes, the argument for invisible things. 2 For by it our elders obtained their testimonial. 3 Through faith we perceive that the ages were ordered by the word of God, so that what is seen has not come about from what is revealed.

[1] For 'foundation', **hypostasis**, see previous notes on 1.3 and 3.14. It should be noted that this word also was used to denote a document proving ownership of property, in other words, a title deed.

This verse is often misunderstood, probably because of the use of the word 'substance', Vulg. *substantia*, to translate **hypostasis**. Our writer is not saying that the existence of faith is in itself proof of the existence of the invisible world, but rather that faith gives one certainty and an argument for believing in the existence of that world. Chrysostom says, 'Faith . . . brings what are not seen to the same full assurance with what are seen.' He goes on to add, 'For instance, the Resurrection has not come, nor does it exist substantially, but hope makes it substantial in our soul.'

[2] The 'testimonial' is that given by scripture, which testifies to their faithfulness.

[3] 'Were ordered', **katêrtisthai**, not 'created' but rather 'furnished' or 'prepared'.

'By the word of God', **rhêmati Theou**, not the pre-existent 'Word', i.e. Christ, or **Logos**. See the note on **rhêma** in 1.3.

'So that what is seen has not come about from what is revealed', means that God has created the world from nothing; in other words, the world ('what is seen') was not created from something already visible ('what is revealed'). One is reminded of the words of the mother who encourages her son to endure torture rather than submit to the king Antiochus and renounce his religion; 'I beg you, child, look at the sky and the earth; see all that is in them and realize that God made them out of nothing, and that man comes into being in the same way' (NEB II Macc. 7.28).

Some commentators take 'not', **mê**, with 'what is revealed', **phainomenôn**, to create the phrase, 'from what is *not* revealed'. In this they have a precedent in Jerome's Vulgate which reads *ut ex invisibilibus visibilia fierent*. Apart from being a violation of the Greek word order, this makes an ambiguous statement which can be taken either as saying that God made what is visible from what was not visible, i.e. not visible because it did not exist, or as implying that God did *not* create everything, because there was already something invisible in existence. This touches precisely the issue which concerned the early church in its opposition to the Gnostics, who denied that the material world was created by God. Chrysostom points out that 'the philosophers expressly say that "nothing comes out of things that are not", being "sensual" (Jude 19)', in other words, they say that everything was created out of something and, therefore, there was always something existing before-hand.

4 By faith Abel offered a fuller sacrifice than Cain to God, and through this was awarded the reputation of

being a just man, with God awarding it to him as a consequence of his gifts, and through this, although he died, he still speaks. 5 By faith Enoch was removed so that he should not see death, and he could not be found, because God had removed him; for, before his removal, it was testified that he had greatly pleased God. 6 Without faith it is impossible to please him greatly; for the one who approaches God must have believed both that he exists, and that he rewards those who seek him out. 7 By faith Noah was warned of things that had not yet been seen, and reverently constructed an ark to save his household. By this means he condemned the world, and became the heir of the righteousness which is according to faith.

[4] The long catalogue of those who displayed faith starts with Abel. Gen. 4.2–4 tells how Abel offered the firstlings of his flock, while Cain offered 'of the fruit of the ground'. There has been much speculation as to why the Lord preferred Abel's offering. Was it because it was early and Cain's was late? Or was it because the sacrifice of a living creature is superior to the offering of produce? Certainly the Jews regarded Abel's offering as the one preferred by God because, according to tradition, fire from heaven consumed his offering.

I have taken **autou** here to mean 'of him', i.e. 'his', going with 'gifts', but it is possible to take it with **tou Theou** and translate it as 'with God *himself . . .*'.

[5] Genesis 5.24 (AV) says, 'And Enoch walked with God: and he was not; for God took him.' This verse was interpreted by Jewish tradition as indicating that Enoch did not die and was taken directly into God's presence. As Montefiore points

out, his earthly life of 365 years was much shorter than his father's (962) or his son's (969), and it was suggested that God translated him to remove him from possible contamination by sin while still (comparatively) young.

[6] Our writer cannot give an example of Enoch's faithfulness, since scripture is silent on that point, so he has to argue from the fact that God took him into his presence. He must have pleased God for this to happen, and as no one who lacks faith can please God, Enoch must have been faithful.

It is interesting to note the definition of 'faith', **pistis**, implied in this verse; firstly, it is belief in God's existence, and secondly, trust in God's grace and goodness. The word has a passive sense, denoting trustworthiness, and an active one, denoting trustfulness. This is also the case with the adjective **pistos**, which means trustworthy (passive), or believing (active). Our word 'faithful' similarly expresses both aspects. A rich range of meanings is carried by the word **pistis**, from intellectual belief to emotional commitment. Trust, obedience, assurance, confidence, even credit in a commercial sense, are all meanings of the word. See the notes on 3.12 and 4.6.

[7] It is easier to see how Noah displayed faith. He believed God when he warned him about the flood, 'things that had not yet been seen', **tôn mêdepô blepomenôn**, and by his example of faithfulness 'condemned the world', because they did not believe.

'Reverently', **eulabêtheis**, literally, 'having shown reverence'. The noun **eulabeia** is used in 5.7 to describe Christ's piety in the face of death.

'Became the heir of the righteousness which is according to faith' reminds one of Gal. 3.24, 'So the law became our minder (**paidagôgos**) for Christ, so that we might be justified through faith.' Noah, too, was justified through his faith.

8 By faith, when called to go out to a place which he was to receive as his inheritance, Abraham obeyed and went out without understanding where he was going. 9 By faith he settled as a foreigner in the land of promise as in a strange land, living in tents with Isaac and Jacob his fellow-heirs of the same promise. 10 For he awaited the city with foundations, whose architect and creator was God. 11 By faith barren Sarah herself received the power to conceive seed, and that when she was past child-bearing age, because she judged the one who made the promise faithful. 12 Hence there sprang from just one man, and that from one who was in this respect virtually dead, as many as the stars of heaven in number and as the innumerable grains of sand on the sea shore.

[8, 9] Genesis 12.1–8 tells how Abraham was ordered by God to leave the land of Haran, and how he entered the land of Canaan where God appeared to him and promised that his seed would inherit the land.

'He settled as a foreigner', **parôikêsen,** i.e. 'lived as an alien', because he knew that he had to move on. The fact that he lived in tents proves his stay was temporary.

[10] 'The city' is the heavenly Jerusalem. 'With foundations' is in contrast to the tents of the previous verse. Note that our writer adds an extra dimension to the original story. Abraham treats his stay in Canaan as temporary, although the land was promised to his descendants, but not on that occasion to him, not because he is awaiting a call to the heavenly city, but because he was journeying further.

'Creator', **dêmiourgos;** a rare use of this word to describe

God. This was the word used by the Gnostics to denote the evil god who created the material world, and its use by our writer would indicate that he was not troubled by this fact, perhaps because he had not had occasion to deal with them, or more probably because he was deliberately re-defining the word.

[11] 'Power to conceive seed', **dynamin eis katabolên spermatos**, literally, 'power for the depositing of seed', would seem to be inappropriate when applied to a woman. It is not difficult, however, to stretch the meaning to include the idea of receiving or putting away the seed so that it might grow. **Katabolê** often means 'foundation' or 'beginning'. There is certainly no need to alter the text.

Genesis 18.12 records Sarah's initial reaction to the news that she would have a son as sceptical: 'Sarah laughed within herself'. We must presume that she later thought better of it.

[12] 'Virtually dead', **nenekrômenou**, literally, 'dead', 'mortified'.

Our writer quotes (with poetical embellishment) Gen. 22.17 (AV), 'That in blessing I will bless thee, and in multiplying I will multiply thy seed as the stars of the heaven, and as the sand which is upon the sea shore.'

13 All these died in faith, although they did not receive the promises, but saw them from afar, and welcomed them, admitting that they were foreigners and aliens on the earth. 14 For those who speak in this way reveal that they are looking for a homeland. 15 And if they had thought about the country they had left, they would have found a chance to turn back. 16 But as it is, they yearn for a better country, that is, a

heavenly one. Therefore God is not ashamed of being called their God; for he has prepared a city for them.

[13] Strictly speaking, not all of these died in faith, if we include Enoch who did not die. Is it also correct to speak of them all as 'foreigners and aliens'? Our writer is thinking primarily of Abraham, Isaac, Jacob and Sarah, and, possibly in anticipation, of Moses. But Abel too, according to tradition, had nowhere to call his own, after he and Cain had agreed to divide the world. Cain took the earth and everything that was stationary. Abel took everything that moved. As a result Abel had nowhere he could stay, and was pursued to his death by Cain. Enoch was so much an alien on this earth that God took him away from it, and Noah too, had to leave his home because of the Flood, and commit himself to a long journey on water.

'Foreigners and aliens', **xenoi kai parepidêmoi,** are to be distinguished by the fact that the former had no rights in the country where they happened to be, while the latter were foreigners with some rights as temporary residents.

[14] 'Speak in this way', i.e. admit they are foreigners in a strange land.

[15, 16] The fact that they do not turn back demonstrates both their faithful obedience to God and their belief in a heavenly homeland.

17 By faith Abraham offered Isaac when tested, and he who had received the promises was offering his only child; 18 to him was uttered the statement, 'In Isaac shall your seed be called'. 19 He reckoned that God was able to raise him even from the dead, from which, figuratively, he did recover him.

[17] We return to Abraham and the supreme example of faith, his offering of Isaac. The imperfect tense, 'was offering', can mean either 'was in the process of offering', or 'began to offer'.

'His only child', **ton monogenê**: this is not strictly true since he had another son, Ishmael. However, as the next verse indicates, Isaac was the only son to be considered as inheriting the promise, after Ishmael and Hagar were sent away, and this would make him the sole heir.

[18] The quotation is from Gen. 21.12. 'To him', i.e. Abraham, or 'in regard to him', i.e. Isaac.

[19] There was a tradition that Isaac's soul left his body as his father's knife was falling. In other words, Isaac actually died. At the words, 'Lay not thine hand upon the lad', Gen. 22.12 (AV), his soul returned. In this way both Abraham and Isaac learned that God would raise the dead. It is not necessary to suppose that this particular tradition was in the mind of our writer.

'Figuratively', **en parabolêi**, because he did not actually die. In other words, it was like a resurrection from the dead. This phrase has led to some speculation. Firstly, it has been suggested that it means the same as **parabolôs**, 'beyond all expectation', or 'in an extraordinary manner'. But there is no evidence for this usage. Finally, it has been translated as 'by the figure' (of the ram). Chrysostom claimed that the substitution of the ram for Isaac made the ram a representation of Isaac. 'By means of the ram he received him again, having slain it in his stead', and then adds cryptically, 'But these things were types: for here it is the Son of God who is slain', suggesting that the ram was also representing the sacrifice of Christ. Although it is a possible interpretation, it is an obscure reference, and reflects the fertile speculations this passage attracted in the early church.

20 By faith Isaac blessed Jacob and Esau, and that in regard to the future as well. 21 By faith Jacob blessed each of Joseph's sons, when he was dying, and bowed down over the top of his staff. 22 By faith Joseph at his end spoke of the departure of the sons of Israel, and gave instructions regarding his bones. 23 By faith Moses, when he was born, was hidden three months by his parents, because they saw that the child was handsome, and they did not respect the king's command. 24 By faith Moses, when he was grown up, refused to be called the son of Pharaoh's daughter, 25 choosing to bear adversity with the people of God, rather than have a temporary enjoyment of sin, 26 judging the insults faced by Christ a greater wealth than the treasures of Egypt, for he was looking at the recompense.

[20–26] The faith of all the persons mentioned in these verses is manifested in their firm belief that God had a plan either for themselves or for those they loved.

[20] Genesis 27.28–29, 39–40 tells the story of the blessing of Jacob and Esau. They both received a blessing for general prosperity and, in regard to their future, Isaac prophesied that Jacob would be the leader of his brethren, while Esau was told he would first serve his brother but later 'have the dominion'.

[21] 'Staff' is a mistranslation in the Septuagint of the Hebrew word which actually means 'bed', Gen. 47.31. Our writer transfers this incident, when only Jacob (otherwise known as Israel) and Joseph were present, to the later blessing of Ephraim and Manasseh recorded in 48.9–14. Chrysostom

regards the bowing as significant; 'inasmuch as another King was about to arise from Ephraim . . . "he bowed himself" to Joseph, showing the obeisance of the whole people which was to be [directed] to him.'

[22] Genesis 50.24–25 is the source of this verse.

[23] 'Handsome', **asteion**, Vulg. *elegantem*. Both the Latin and Greek carry the double meanings, 1. 'intelligent' or 'witty', 2. 'handsome' or 'fine'. The slang word 'cute' is the nearest we have to this. Exodus 2.2 (AV) says, 'she saw him that he was a goodly child'.

'The king's command', i.e. that all male children were to be killed. See Ex. 1.16.

[24] 'Refused to be called the son of Pharaoh's daughter', because he defended an Israelite and killed the Egyptian who was assaulting him, Ex. 2.11–12.

[26] 'The insults faced by Christ' are compared with those of Moses. Chrysostom defines them as insulting treatment and ingratitude on the part of those one is trying to help. Exodus 2.14 (AV) describes the reaction when Moses tried to stop an Israelite attacking another one, and the aggressor replied, 'Who made thee a prince and a judge over us? Intendest thou to kill me, as thou killedst the Egyptian?' It has been suggested that 'Christ', literally, 'the anointed', here stands for 'the chosen people', but it would be a unique example of this usage in the NT.

27 By faith he left Egypt unafraid of the king's anger; for he persevered as though he saw the unseen one. 28 By faith he kept the passover and the pouring out of the

blood, so that he who was destroying the first-born should not touch them. 29 By faith they crossed the Red Sea as though over dry land, but when the Egyptians tried to do this they were swallowed up.

[27] The first time Moses left Egypt to take refuge in Midian (Ex. 2.15), he is described as being afraid. Chrysostom, who takes the verse as referring to this incident, explains the expression 'unafraid' by referring to Moses' willingness to present himself to Pharaoh on a later occasion. On the other hand, does it refer to the Exodus from Egypt, when he led the Israelites into the wilderness? It would certainly be a more appropriate description, although it is out of chronological order in this passage. It is possible to take **mê phobêtheis**, translated here as 'unafraid', as meaning 'not respecting', i.e. 'scorning', as in v. 23, where our translation says of Moses' parents that 'they did not respect', **ouk ephobêthêsan**, literally, 'they did not fear'.

'As though he saw the unseen one', namely, the King of Heaven. In other words, Moses obeyed the king he could not see rather than the one he could see.

[28] This is described in Ex. 12.

[29] See Ex. 14.26–27. The fact that the Egyptians were drowned does not prove that they lacked faith. Our writer is not comparing their faith with that of Moses. The point is that Moses had faith in God when he was instructed to stretch out his hand and make the water return.

30 By faith the walls of Jericho fell when surrounded for seven days. 31 By faith Rahab the prostitute did not perish along with those who disbelieved, when she had

received the spies in peace. 32 And what more shall I say? For the time would fail me to tell of Gideon, Barak, Samson, Jephthah, of David and Samuel and the prophets, 33 who, through faith, conquered kingdoms, dispensed justice, won promises, stopped the mouths of lions, 34 quenched the power of fire, escaped the edge of the sword, were empowered out of weakness, became strong in war and turned aside the armies of the aliens.

[30] See Josh. 6 for the source of this reference.

[31] Joshua 2.1–21 tells how Rahab received the two Israelite spies, and, accepting their statement that God had given them the land, hid them from the king of Jericho. 'Those who disbelieved', **tois apeithêsâsin**, literally 'those who disobeyed' (Vulg. *incredulis*), refers to the ones who did not accept that God had given the Israelites their land or that the God of the Israelites was to be obeyed. The verb **apeitheô**, which corresponds to the noun **apeitheia** (see note on 4.6), also means 'to be faithless'. Rahab displayed her faith by believing not only that the Israelites had been singled out by God due to his treatment of them in the wilderness, but also that, as Josh. 2.11 (AV) puts it, 'the Lord your God, he is God in heaven above, and in earth beneath'.

One might have expected the story of Rahab to come before the fall of Jericho. The reason it is mentioned after the fall of the city may be because it is recalled in Josh. 6.25, i.e. after the collapse of the walls recounted earlier in the chapter.

[32] Gideon won a victory over the Midianites (Judges 7), Barak was the ally of Deborah the prophetess, and defeated the

Canaanite Sisera (Judges 4), Samson's exploits are recounted in Judges 13–16, Jephthah defeated the Ammonites (Judges 11.1–33), and the stories of David and Samuel are told in both books of Samuel.

'The prophets' are not named here, unless we include Samuel among them.

[33] Those who 'conquered kingdoms' include Gideon, Jephthah and David; those who 'dispensed justice' would include Samuel and David; and the candidates for (permanently) stopping the 'mouths of lions' are Samson and David. We should also include Daniel, although in the latter's case the credit for stopping the lions' mouths should go to the angel and no lion was killed (Dan. 6.22).

The 'promises' must be of land or inheritances, not the heavenly promise referred to in v. 39.

[34] Shadrach, Meshach and Abednego 'quenched the power of fire' (Dan. 3). They are not strictly prophets, but their story is told in the book of the prophet Daniel.

Several of those mentioned, and many who have not been mentioned, 'escaped the edge of the sword', or 'became strong in war and turned aside the armies of the aliens'. Samson is the one who springs to mind as 'empowered out of weakness', but Chrysostom thinks that this is a reference to the return of the Jews after their captivity in Babylon.

35 Women received their dead after resurrection, others were beaten, refusing to be bought off, in order to gain a better resurrection. 36 Others again were tried by mocking and whipping, and also bonds and imprisonment. 37 They were stoned, sawn in two, died in slaughter by the sword, went around in sheep skins

and goat skins, destitute, afflicted and maltreated, 38 of whom the world was not worthy, wandering in deserts, mountains, caves and holes in the ground. 39, 40 And all of these won their reputation through their faith, but, since God had something better in view for us, did not gain the promise, in order that they should not be perfected without us.

[35] The two examples of resurrection which one might recall are those recorded in I Kings 17.17–24, the widow's son whom Elijah revived, and in II Kings 4.18–37, the child of the Shunammite whom Elisha raised from the dead.

'Were beaten', **etympanisthêsan**, from **tympanon**, 'drum'. It has been suggested that the word means 'were stretched on a wheel', but the evidence for this is slight, although there was an instrument of torture known as a **tympanon**, which was probably used as a whipping frame.

'Refusing to be bought off', **ou prosdexamenoi tên apoly-trôsin. Apolytrôsis** is literally a release on payment of a ransom. The case of Eleazer (II Macc. 6.18–31), who refused to eat pork and was flogged to death, the penalty for those who refused to conform, is apposite. The officials in charge of the feast had privately encouraged him to bring his own kosher meat to the feast, and merely pretend to be eating the pork. Eleazer, however, refused to act deceitfully and died for his principles. The story told in the next chapter, II Macc. 7, of the seven brothers similarly tortured to death for refusing to eat pork must also have been in the mind of our writer.

[36] Cases of 'mocking' or 'whipping' can be found in various passages of the OT and the Apocrypha, particularly Maccabees. The fate of Jeremiah, who suffered both forms of

punishment (Jer. 20.2), and later 'bonds' and 'imprisonment' (Jer. 38.6), is perhaps the example this verse recalls.

[37] Zechariah (II Chron. 24.21) was stoned to death by king Joash. Chrysostom also instances the stoning of Stephen, but this cannot be appropriate in a list of pre-Christian martyrs.

'Sawn in two', **epristhêsan**, is the best reading. Some manuscripts have **epeirâsthêsan**, 'were tempted', probably because the word **epristhêsan** was unfamiliar. Some scholars have suggested **epyrôthêsan** or **eprêsthêsan**, 'were burned', but there is no justification for these amendments. Although there is no mention in the OT of any such martyrdom, in II Sam. 12.31 we read that David 'put under saws' (AV), or as the Sept. has it, **ethêken en tôi prioni**, literally, 'he placed on the saw', the inhabitants of Rabbah. There was, however, a strong tradition amongst the rabbis and early Christian writers that Isaiah was sawn apart by king Manasseh.

Examples of the faithful who 'died by the sword' are not hard to find. Elijah in I Kings 19.10 (AV) complains that the children of Israel have 'slain thy prophets with the sword'.

Both Elijah and Elisha fit the description of those who 'went around in sheep skins', and were 'destitute, afflicted and maltreated', but our writer is probably also thinking of the Maccabean freedom fighters. Certainly the 'deserts, mountains, caves and holes in the ground' of the next verse were the background of their operations.

[38] 'The world', **kosmos**, according to Chrysostom, includes the people and creation itself. 'If the whole creation, with the human beings that belong to it, were put in the balance, they yet would not be of equal value with these; and with reason. For as ten thousand measures of chaff and hay would not be of equal value to ten pearls, so neither [would] they.'

[39, 40] 'Won their reputation', **martyrêthentes**, literally, 'having been testified', i.e. by scripture. See the note on 11.2.

Although the faithful of the OT and the Apocrypha 'did not gain the promise' at the time, it is clear from the following clause, 'in order that they should not be perfected *without us* (**chôris hêmôn**)', that our writer believes that they *will* inherit the promise and be perfected along with the Christian faithful. For 'perfected', see notes on 2.10, 5.9 and 10.14.

Chapter 12

1 Therefore, since we have so great a cloud of witnesses surrounding us, let us too put away every encumbrance and insidious sin, and run with patience the race that lies before us, 2 looking towards the pioneer and perfecter of our faith, Jesus, who in place of the joy that lay before him, endured the cross, scorning the shame, and is seated at the right hand of the throne of God.

[1] 'Cloud of witnesses', **nephos martyrôn**, refers to the roll-call of the previous chapter, and we can see how the word for 'witness' came to give us the word 'martyr', since they all suffered, many to the point of death, for their faith. Chrysostom seems to take the word **ongkon**, translated here as 'encumbrance', but also meaning 'weight' or 'load', as applying to the 'cloud of witnesses'. As a consequence he has to assume that the object of 'put away' is 'everything', **panta** (neuter plural rather than masculine accusative singular agreeing with **ongkon**).

'Insidious', **euperistaton**, an adjective coming from a verb **periistamai**, 'surround', 'encircle' or 'ambush'. Chrysostom explains the adjective as meaning either 'that which easily surrounds us' or the opposite, 'that which can easily be circumvented'. The word, unfortunately, is not used elsewhere and so we cannot be definite about its precise meaning here, but on balance 'easily circumventing' seems to be more appropriate than 'easily circumvented', and is certainly suggested by Jerome's translation *circumstans*. Chrysostom, however, prefers the latter interpretation, adding, 'for it is easy, if we will, to overcome sin'. One early manuscript has a variant reading, **euperispaston**, 'easy to pull away', which would support Chrysostom's interpretation.

[2] 'Perfecter', **teleiôtên**, i.e. one who completes or finishes a task. There is no evidence to support Moffatt's translation, 'perfect embodiment'. Our writer is saying that Christ, who led the way, is the one who will see us safely to the end of that road.

'In place of', **anti**, implies that Christ voluntarily undertook the death on the cross, when he could have avoided it. Before his incarnation the son of God enjoyed eternal bliss, but he laid that aside in order to save us from sin and death. As Montefiore says, this passage refers to the 'joy of eternal sonship in heaven which Jesus renounced in order to endure a cross'. **Anti**, however, can also mean 'for the sake of' or 'in return for', but if this were the sense implied here, the writer would be saying that Christ was motivated by pleasure when he chose to endure the crucifixion. It would also be irrelevant, as the argument is that we, too, must lay aside easy pleasures in order to follow Jesus. Philippians 2.6 is appropriate to quote on this subject: 'Who being in the form of God did not treat his equality with God as *an excuse for self indulgence* (**harpagmon**, literally, 'booty' or 'a lucky find').'

3 For consider the one who endured such opposition directed against him by sinners, so that your hearts may not faint or be weary. 4 As yet, you have not resisted to the point of shedding blood in your struggle

against sin. 5 And you have forgotten the appeal which is addressed to you as his sons, 'My son, do not despise the Lord's discipline, nor faint when you are tested by him; 6 for the Lord disciplines the one he loves, and whips every son he receives.'

[3] 'Consider', or rather 'consider and compare', **analogisas-the.**

'Against himself', **eis heauton.** Some manuscripts have **heautous,** 'themselves', or **autous,** 'them', but it is difficult to see what such a text can mean. Both Chrysostom and Jerome (Vulg. *semetipsum*) take **heauton** as the correct reading.

[4] There is no need to assume that this verse must pre-date the Neronian persecution of 64, or that our writer must be addressing a group who did not live in Rome. In the first place, the people our writer is addressing could have survived such a persecution, since they have admittedly not 'shed blood'. Secondly, it is likely that not all members of the Christian church in Rome suffered persecution, especially if they were regarded by their pagan neighbours as Jewish rather than Christian.

[5, 6] 'Appeal', **paraklêsis,** or 'exhortation'. The text is from Prov. 3.11, 12. Verse 12 in the Septuagint version quoted here is markedly different from the Hebrew. In the AV it reads, 'For whom the Lord loveth he correcteth; *even as a father the son in whom he delighteth.*'

The noun 'discipline' in 5, and also in 7 and 8, is **paideia,** usually translated as 'education' or 'training'. The corresponding verb, which is used in vv. 6 and 7, is **paideuo.** Both are derived from the word for 'child', **pais.** There is an association in Greek between childhood and education, which we miss in the English translation.

7 Be patient when it comes to discipline; God treats you as sons. For what son does a father not discipline? 8 If you lack the discipline which all have shared, then you are illegitimate and not [true] sons. 9 Besides, we had earthly fathers who disciplined us, and we showed them respect; shall we not much more subject ourselves to our spiritual Father and live? 10 For they used to discipline us for a short time, and as they saw fit, but he [does it] for our benefit, and so that we should share his holiness. 11 All discipline is regarded at the time as not delightful but distressing. Later, however, it yields the fruit of peace and righteousness to those who have been trained through it.

[7–11] This passage presents great difficulty to many modern readers. In his commentary, which was published in 1964, Montefiore made the following observation: 'The ancient world did not feel the problem of evil with the same intensity as the modern world just because its "father image" was different . . . It was not until ideas of liberal education began to have currency, and the value of corporal punishment and the inculcation of fear began to be questioned, that the full force of the theological problems concerning human suffering began to be felt.'

Thirty years later one might reflect how much wider still is the gulf between the modernist and the traditionalist stance, particularly in reference to the institutions of marriage and the family, and not just to patriarchy.

[9] 'Earthly', literally, 'of the flesh', **tês sarkos,** contrasts our

human fathers with our heavenly Father, described here as 'the father of [our]spirits', **tôi patri tôn pneumatôn**.

The notion that human fathers were counterparts of our heavenly Father is found also in Eph. 3.14–15, 'For this reason I bow my knees before the Father, **patera**, after whom every family, **patriâ** (literally, 'descent on the father's side' or 'fatherhood', Vulg. *paternitas*), in heaven and on earth is named.'

[10] 'As they saw fit', or 'according to their opinions', which can be mistaken or even selfish, in contrast with God's will, which always aims at our perfection.

[11] 'Fruit of peace and righteousness', literally, 'peaceful fruit of righteousness', **karpon eirênikon dikaiosynês**, expresses both the peace between God and a human being when a state of righteousness is attained, and also the calm which follows the struggle and stress of training. The athletic metaphor is deliberate, as 'trained' in this verse translates **gegymnasmenois** from the verb **gymnazomai**, which denotes stripping to exercise in a **gymnasion**.

12 Therefore, straighten the arms that hang limp and the knees that are feeble, 13 and make straight paths for your feet, so that what is lame should be healed rather than turned aside. 14 Pursue peace with all and holiness, without which none shall see the Lord, 15 watching out lest anyone fall short of God's grace, lest some bitter root sprout up and cause trouble, and through it the majority be tainted, 16 lest there be some fornicator or unprincipled person like Esau, who sold his birthright for one piece of food. 17 For you

know that even when he later wished to inherit his blessing, he was rejected, for he did not obtain an opportunity for going back on his decision, although he sought it with tears.

[12] This verse is a close paraphrase of Isa. 35.3 (Sept.), 'Be strong, you slack (**aneimenai**) arms, and feeble knees'. Closer still to our writer's vocabulary is Ecclus. 25.23, 'arms that hang limp (**pareimenai**) and feeble knees'.

[13] 'Turned aside', **ektrapêi**, or, according to Montefiore, 'dislocated'.

[14] Moffatt translates the first part of this verse, 'along with everybody pursue peace'. It is, however, more likely that our writer is expressing the same thought as Paul in Rom. 12.18, 'As far as you can, live in peace with all people', rather than exhorting his audience to join some universal peace movement.

[15] 'Fall short', or 'hang back', since the Greek verb **hystereô** can carry the sense of arriving late or delaying. See the note on 4.1.
  'Bitter root', i.e. a poisonous weed.

[16] 'Fornicator', **pornos,** is often used in the OT to denote anybody who is incontinent or sensual in a wider sense than the simply sexual.
  'Unprincipled', **bebêlos**, literally, 'that which can be trodden on', 'profane', hence 'impure'.

[17] 'Opportunity for going back on his decision', **topon metanoiâs**, i.e. 'a place of repentance'. Esau wanted to go back on his bargain with Joseph.

18 For you have not come to something you can feel, ablaze with fire, darkness, gloom, a tempest, 19 the blare of a trumpet and the sound of words, which, when they heard, they begged that no more be said to them. 20 For they could not bear what was being commanded (if even an animal should touch the mountain, it was to be stoned to death), 21 and so frightening was the sight that Moses said, 'I am terrified and I tremble'. 22 But you have come to mount Sion and the city of the living God, the heavenly Jerusalem, and hosts of angels celebrating, 23 and the assembly of the first-born enrolled in heaven, and God the Judge of all, and the spirits of the righteous made perfect, 24 and Jesus the mediator of the new covenant, and the blood of purification speaking more forcefully than Abel's.

[18, 19] 'Something', i.e. a mountain. There is no noun in the original, unless the noun intended as the object of the main verb is 'fire'. Some manuscripts add **orei**, 'mountain', and it is clear that Mount Sinai is meant and is here contrasted with the heavenly Sion. In Galatians 4 Paul makes the same comparison of the earthly Sinai, the place of the old covenant, with the heavenly Jerusalem, the place of the new covenant.

'You can feel', literally, 'being handled', **psêlaphômenôi**, that is, capable of being apprehended by the physical senses. The same verb is used in I John 1.1, 'and our hands *have handled* (**epsêlaphêsan**)', to express the material reality of the incarnate Word. It can be used to denote more than simply touching.

Deuteronomy 4.11 and 5.22, 25 clearly are sources of these verses. Exodus 19.16 also seems to be recalled, since it provides the reference to the trumpet with the sentence (Sept.), **phônê tês salpingos êchei mega**, 'the sound of the trumpet blared aloud'.

'They begged that no more be said' is based on Deut. 5.25 (Sept.), 'if we continue to hear the voice of the Lord our God any longer, we shall even die'. The use of the verb **prostithêmi**, 'repeat' or 'continue', in both passages points to the connection.

[20] 'Stoned to death' is followed in some manuscripts by 'or shot by a javelin', because the phrase occurs in the Sept. version of Ex. 19.13, on which this verse is based.

[21] 'I am terrified' was actually said by Moses on the occasion he came down from Sinai to find that the people had made a golden calf (Deut. 9.19), not on the occasion described in this passage. 'I tremble' seems to be an addition by the writer. It could be that he is using a source which is not scriptural.

[22] 'You have come', **proselêlythate**, a verb repeated from v. 18, contrasts with the unapproachable mount Sinai. Furthermore, it expresses the amazing truth that the believer of the new covenant has already in some mysterious way been admitted to the joys of heaven. We have been given direct access (**parrhêsiâ**) to God by the mediation of Christ. Our worship here below is not taking part in a separate place but is caught up with and shares in the worship of those in heaven.

There is no justification for translating this verb as 'you have drawn near to', and saying along with Montefiore, 'His readers have not yet actually arrived at Mount Zion: they have drawn close.' Of course our writer is aware that the race has not yet been run and the final goal is still to be gained. He has repeatedly made this very point throughout the letter. This does not, however, invalidate the fact that the Christian while still on earth worships God in the company of angels and all the faithful and is already a citizen of the heavenly Jerusalem.

'Hosts of angels celebrating', **mûriasin angelôn panêgyrei**, Vulg. *multorum milium angelorum frequentiam*. **Panêgyrei** denotes an assembly of worshippers on a festive occasion. As Chrysostom points out, this joy and delight contrasts with the gloom and darkness of Sinai.

[23] 'The assembly of the first-born' must refer to the angels, because they were created before man. If the 'first-born' were human beings, the phrase 'the spirits of the righteous made perfect' would be redundant. Nor can the latter phrase refer back to the first, since it is separated by 'God the Judge of all'. It is more likely that 'the righteous' are the faithful patriarchs and prophets recalled in the previous chapter and probably also the Christian faithful who have departed. Ignatius, in his letter to the Philadelphians (9.1), speaking of Jesus, the high priest entrusted with the Holy of Holies, says, 'being himself the Father's door, through which enter Abraham, Isaac, Jacob, the prophets, the apostles and the church'.

[24] Jesus is linked to the human beings of the previous verse as God is linked to the angels, and this link is underlined by the references to the mediator of the new covenant and the blood of his sacrifice, through which man can enter heaven.

'More forcefully', **kreitton**, rather than 'better', because, while it is true to say that the blood of Jesus has a better message to deliver than that of Abel, namely, reconciliation rather than vengeance, **kreitton** conveys the sense of superiority, sovereignty and power. 'With more authority' would be an alternative translation.

25 See that you do not refuse him who speaks; for, if those who had refused the one who spoke a warning

on earth did not escape, much less shall we, who abandon the one [speaking] from heaven. 26 His voice then shook the earth, but now he has promised saying, 'One more time shall I make not only the earth to quake but also heaven'. 27 'One more time' points to the removal of what is shaken, namely of what was created, so that what is not shaken should remain. 28 Therefore, seeing that we are receiving an unshakeable kingdom, let us hold on to grace, so that we might through it offer God a pleasing worship with reverence and fear. 29 For indeed, our God is a consuming fire.

[25] Our writer returns to the theme that runs through the letter; the avoidance of apostasy.

'Who speaks' picks up the reference to Christ in the previous verse. But can we assume that 'the one [speaking] from heaven' also refers to Christ? If we did not supply 'speaking' in the second reference, this would be the obvious conclusion. It is better, however, to take 'the one [speaking] from heaven' as being a reference to God the Father, who spoke twice from heaven: firstly, on the occasion of Jesus' baptism by John (Matt. 3.17 [AV], 'and lo a voice from heaven, saying, This is my beloved Son, in whom I am well pleased'); and secondly, at the Transfiguration (Matt. 17.5 [AV], 'and behold a voice out of the cloud, which said, This is my beloved Son, in whom I am well pleased; hear ye him'). If we take 'the one [speaking] from heaven' as referring to the Father, the next verse presents no difficulty, since it clearly is also a reference to the Father.

'The one who spoke a warning on earth' is Moses, rather than God speaking on Sinai. The disobedience of the Israelites consisted in refusing to accept what Moses said. The writer always contrasts Moses, not God, as the mediator of the old covenant with Christ the mediator of the new. Furthermore, the use of the verb translated here as 'who spoke a warning', **chrêmatizonta,** often can denote giving a response or instructions when an oracle has been consulted, and would indicate the mediator Moses rather than God who communicated through him. The addition of the phrase 'on earth' would also point to Moses. The manuscripts show some variation in word order at this point and one version of the text allows us, although there seems to be little advantage in doing so, to translate this section as 'if those who had refused on earth the one who spoke a warning did not escape'.

[26] 'His voice then shook the earth', as I argue above, must refer to God speaking on Sinai. In Greek this is more obvious than it is in English because, literally translated, it means, '*whose* voice then shook the earth', and the relative has to refer to 'the one speaking from heaven'. The text quoted is from Hagg. 2.6, with the addition of 'not only' and 'but also' and a variation in word order.

[27] 'One more time', **eti hapax,** i.e the last time, when the world will be destroyed.

'What is not shaken', **ta mê saleuomena,** the new creation or the heavenly kingdom referred to in the next verse.

Gregory of Nazianzus (*Speeches,* 5.25) says, 'There have been two remarkable transitions of life, which are also called earthquakes because of their amazing nature; the first from idols to the law, the second from the law to the gospel. We bring the good news of yet a third earthquake, the transition from the present order to the future, the transition hence to that which is there, that is, to what is no longer moved *nor shaken* (**mêde saleuomena**).'

[28] 'Seeing that we are receiving', **paralambanontes,** is a present participle. In other words, we are in the process of

receiving the kingdom, because we only come into full possession when we have completed the course, or when Christ returns in glory.

'Let us hold on to grace', **echômen charin**, which means more than 'let us keep the state of grace we enjoy now'. The Greek can mean, 'let us give thanks', and this is the interpretation favoured by Chrysostom, although **charis** never carries this sense in the cases where it occurs in our letter. It also seems likely that our writer is asking his audience to do more than simply be grateful. It is their faithful adherence that he demands.

Charis is a difficult word. We are used to translating it as 'grace', from the Latin *gratia*, but the root meaning in the NT is 'a free gift' or 'a blessing', something given by God, not as a reward for merit, but out of his love and to the undeserving. The word is related to **charisma**, which is illustrated in I Cor. 12.4–11, where Paul emphasizes the role of the Holy Spirit in bestowing spiritual **charismata** on all Christians. Apostasy would involve refusing or handing back the free gift of God. Hence to remain loyal, we must hold on to the gift. It is interesting to note that the over-used terms 'charisma' and 'charismatic' derive from this word.

'Reverence', **eulabeiâs** (see notes on 5.7 and 11.7); 'fear', **deous**. There are variant readings, but they are not crucially different from the text adopted here.

[29] This comes from Deut. 4.24, a passage which appropriately describes the reaction of God to unfaithfulness.

Chapter 13

1 Let brotherly love continue. 2 Do not forget hospitality, for through this some have entertained angels unawares. 3 Remember prisoners as though you were imprisoned with them, and those in distress as though you, too, were in their bodies.

[1] 'Brotherly love', **philadelphiâ,** should be understood as affection between fellow Christians rather than general philanthropy, since it denotes love between brothers and sisters; in other words, family.

[2] Famous cases of hosts entertaining angels include the story in Gen. 18 of Abraham and the three traditionally identified as angels, who prophesied that Sarah would have a son, and the story in Gen. 19 of Lot and the two angels he entertained in Sodom. In Tobit the whole plot depends on the fact that Tobit and Tobias do not realize that their guest is an angel until he chooses to reveal it.

[3] 'As though you were imprisoned with them', or 'as having been prisoners yourselves'. The former is preferable, since it is not likely that all his audience had been in prison.

'Those in distress', **kakouchoumenôn;** 'as though you, too, were in their bodies', **hôs kai autoi ontes en sômati,** literally, 'as also yourselves being in body'. There are other interpretations. Firstly, 'since you yourselves are also in the body of the church' (or 'of Christ'), and secondly, 'since you too are in the body', i.e. 'since you too have bodies'. The first interpretation is obscure and stretches the text too far, although the notion of the church as the body of Christ is familiar from other references in the NT, and the second, although an unusual concept, is possible. Philo, however, in a passage describing the reaction of people witnessing the torture of their friends and relatives (*Special Laws*, 3.161), uses the phrase, 'as though suffering themselves in the bodies of others', **hôs en tois heterôn sômasin autoi kakoumenoi.** This is so close to the phrase used by our writer that we must assume that he, too, is speaking of the experience of empathy.

4 Marriage [is] to be respected by everyone, and the marriage bed [is] not to be defiled, for God will judge fornicators and adulterers. 5 [Let your] way of life [be] free of the love of money; [be] content with what you have. For he has said, 'I will not let you go nor abandon you.' 6 So we should have the confidence to say, 'The Lord is my helper, and I shall not fear. What shall people do to me?' 7 Remember those who were your leaders, who spoke to you the word of God, and imitate their faith as you recall the final outcome of their way of life.

[4] This carefully structured verse deserves a detailed analysis.

Firstly, 'marriage (is) to be respected', **tîmios ho gamos**, is aimed at the 'fornicators'. In other words, the institution of marriage is, as the Book of Common Prayer says, 'an honourable estate'. It goes on to say, as some may recollect, 'It was ordained for a remedy against sin, and to avoid fornication.'

'By everyone', or 'among all', **en pâsin,** is not to be taken as meaning that everybody has to get married. There is no hint that our writer is concerned that everyone should be married. It is more likely that he is countering an asceticism which saw the state of marriage as undesirable, if not actually sinful. Some commentators, incidentally, translate **en pâsin** as 'in every way'.

The second part, 'the marriage bed (is) not to be defiled', **hê koitê amiantos,** is aimed at the 'adulterers'. **Koitê** should not be translated simply as 'sex' or 'sexual intercourse', because that might imply that our writer is saying that sex *in itself* is innocent. He is not discussing whether sex in general is good or bad but rather warning his audience against the particular sins of fornication and adultery.

[5] The words quoted are from Deut. 31.6, since Gen. 28.15 and Josh. 1.5, although similar, have a different vocabulary in the Sept. version.

[6] 'Have the confidence to say', **tharrountas legein,** literally, 'to say being bold'.

The quotation is from Psalm 118.6.

[7] It is clear that the leaders referred to are dead, firstly, because the audience are exhorted to remember them and imitate their faithfulness; secondly, because the 'outcome of their way of life', **ekbasin tês anastrophês,** must refer to their death, which is seen as the result of their Christian way of life. Although our writer uses the present participle **hêgoumenoi,** i.e. 'those leading', it is simply a synonym for **hêgemones,** 'leaders'. In other words, we would be entitled to conclude that they are martyrs. If the audience were living in Rome, and this letter was written after the Neronian persecution, their leaders would have included Peter and Paul. They were certainly the

ones 'who spoke to you the word of God', an expression which indicates that they were apostles or evangelists.

8 Jesus Christ is the same, yesterday, today and for ever. 9 Do not be led astray by any subtle and strange teachings; for it is good for the heart to be strengthened by grace, not foods that did not help those who had recourse to them. 10 We have an altar from which those who worship at the tabernacle have no right to eat.

[8] This verse has to be taken with the following verse. Because Jesus does not change, your doctrine should not change.

[9] This is a reference to Jewish dietary laws. But why are such teachings described as 'strange', **xenais**, if our audience is Jewish? Because they are alien and foreign to the new church, being inappropriate, out-dated and unnecessary (see 9.10). It has been suggested that certain Gnostic teachings regarding ascetic diets were creeping into the church, perhaps anticipating later Manichee doctrines in regard to vegetarianism. Clearly, however, our writer refers to past practices, since the tense of the verb 'did not help' (literally, 'were not helped'), **ouk ôphelêthêsan**, rules out any reference to some new teaching. The fact that the word for 'foods', **brômasin**, is used (in the singular) by Paul to refer to pagan offerings in I Cor. 8 is immaterial. The same word occurs in 9.10 of our letter to refer to foods allowed by Jewish dietary laws. **Brôma** is a neutral word for 'food'.

Moffatt's notion that it refers to some view of the eucharist as 'an eating of the body of Christ' should be rejected out of hand, and not just because it faces the same objection as the hypothesis postulating some new Gnostic dietary practice, i.e. our writer is referring to *the past*. Those interested in Moffatt's views might read the passage in his commentary which contains the following: 'In real Christian worship there is no sacrificial meal; the Christian sacrifice is not one of which the worshippers partake by eating', and 'The writer has a mystical or idealistic bent, to which the sacramental idea is foreign. He never alludes to the eucharist; the one sacrament he notices is baptism', and 'The Christian sacrifice on which all our relationship depends, is not one that involves or allows any connection with a meal'.

Our writer uses here a word that is very difficult to pin down. 'Subtle', **poikilais**, meant originally something like 'many-coloured', 'embroidered', hence, 'cunningly made', 'complicated'. This led on to 'diverse', 'various' (as in 2.4), 'intricate', 'subtle'. Finally, 'wily', 'abstruse', 'complex'. What a marvellous word!

[10] 'Altar', **thysiastêrion**, from **thysiâ**, 'sacrifice'. This is the term used in Jewish and Christian contexts, since the normal Greek word for a pagan altar is **bômos**, a word used by Paul when referring to the altar dedicated to the Unknown God in Athens (Acts 17.23). Montefiore says, 'he is referring not to the altar but the victim upon it', but it is clear that this is a reference to the Lord's Table from which the bread of the eucharist was eaten. It should not be taken either as a reference to Calvary; indeed it is repugnant to speak of eating Christ's body off the cross or at Golgotha.

There is a good example of this use of **thysiastêrion** to denote the eucharistic table in Ignatius' letter to the Philadelphians (4), which deserves to be quoted in full. 'So take care to use one eucharist; for there is one flesh of our lord Jesus Christ and one cup for union (**eis henôsin**) of his blood, one altar (**thysiastêr-ion**), as there is one bishop with the presbytery and the deacons, my fellow servants; so that, whatever you do, you may do it according to God.' It should be remembered that this letter was written probably only forty years after the letter to the Hebrews. Even the Puritan Richard Baxter (*Christian Institutes* I, p.304) says of this verse, 'And the naming of the table an altar, as related to the representative sacrifice, is no more improper than the other (i.e. calling our bodies, alms and prayers, sacrifices). "We have an altar whereof they have no right to eat" seems plainly to mean the Sacramental Communion.'

The key word is 'eat', **phagein**, since the Jewish sin-offering was burned and not eaten. Our writer is clearly distinguishing between Jewish and Christian practices.

Those who 'worship at the tabernacle', **hoi têi skênêi latreuontes,** are those who still worship at the Temple in Jerusalem, or (if this was written after the destruction of the Temple) those Jews who still attempt to observe the Mosaic Law.

Finally, if they have 'no right to eat', it follows that we do have that right. In other words, for our writer, eating from the 'altar' is the mark of the Christian believer.

11 For the bodies of the animals whose blood is taken into the sanctuary for a sin-offering by the high priest are burned outside the camp. 12 Accordingly, Jesus, too, suffered outside the gate, in order to sanctify the people through his own blood. 13 Therefore let us go out to him outside the camp, bearing his disgrace. 14 For here we have no continuing city, but are looking for the one that will be. 15 So let us through him offer up a sacrifice of praise continuously to God, that is, the fruit of lips acknowledging his name.

[11] The burning of the sin-offering is mentioned in Lev. 6.23

and 30, but our writer is referring to Lev. 16.27, which adds more detail and refers to the burning 'outside the camp', **exô tês parembolês**. **Parembolê**, which occurs in the plural in 11.34 and is translated there as 'armies', originally denoted a company of soldiers and hence a military encampment. We are reminded that this ordinance was initiated while the Israelites were encamped in the desert. Confusingly, some sacrificial meat was eaten on occasion by the priests, but it is clear that our writer is speaking of the sacrifice of the Day of Atonement.

[12] It might be useful to sum up what the writer has already said about the differences between the new and the old sacrifices. In the first place, we eat sacramentally from the new victim; they burned their victim. Secondly, our sacrifice is once and for all time, but theirs has to be repeated. Now he adds a third difference, namely, that our victim was sacrificed outside the gate, i.e. outside the camp, and theirs was sacrificed in the Holy Place. Finally, our victim is God himself, who gives his own blood, while they sacrificed animals.

The use of the word 'accordingly', **dio**, at the start of this verse indicates that Jesus' sacrifice outside the camp fulfilled the passage of scripture quoted previously; he is the true sacrifice of which the animals sacrificed according to the old dispensation are merely types.

[13, 14] 'His disgrace' was not just that he was outside the camp, but also that he was crucified. Hence in using the expression 'bearing (**pherontes**) his disgrace', the writer is reminding his audience that the Christian is required to take up his cross and follow Jesus.

'Going outside the camp' is to be understood on several levels. Firstly, it differentiates the Jew and the Christian, especially the Jewish Christian who gave up so much of his inheritance and the cultural ties that bound him to an established and ancient religious tradition with its rituals and a spiritual centre in Jerusalem.

Secondly, the Christian was required to go out and evangelize among people who were often rejected by society, the poor and the slaves, and, in the case of a Jewish Christian, to go out into the Gentile world and mix with pagans, in itself a form of pollution. It should be noted that Paul (I Cor. 5.12,13; Col. 4.5; I Thess. 4.12) speaks of 'those outside', **hoi exô**, when he wishes to refer to the unbelievers.

Thirdly, as v. 14 makes clear, he had to turn his back on all earthly cities, being a citizen of the heavenly Jerusalem, his only true home. This severing of all earthly ties, which was seen by the prosecuting authorities as a hatred of mankind, and even a form of atheism, marked the Christian as a danger and a threat to civilized society.

[15] 'Sacrifice of praise', **thysiân aineseôs**, from Ps. 49.23 (Sept.), which is Ps. 50 in the A V (the different numbering is due to the fact that Ps. 9 in the Septuagint is made up of the two Hebrew psalms 9 and 10). The phrase is a paradox blunted by over-familiarity. Instead of sacrificing animals we are required to offer praise instead. The metaphor continues with the reference to 'fruit of lips' below. It recalls the rabbinical saying, 'in the time of the Messiah, all sacrifices will cease, but the sacrifice of thanksgiving will not cease; all prayers will cease, but praises will not cease'.

'Acknowledging' is a better translation than 'praising' of **homologountôn**, which is based on the Sept. version of Ps. 53.8 (54.6 in the A V). Note that the verses in the psalm are also divided differently in the Sept. version. The Greek translation of the text in the psalm goes, 'I shall acknowledge (confess), **exomologêsomai**, your name, Lord, that it is good'. The A V reads, 'I will praise thy name, O Lord; for it is good'.

'Fruit of lips', from the Sept. version of Hosea 14.3 (A V

14.2, where the Hebrew is rendered as 'calves of our lips', although the best text reads 'the fruit of bullocks').

16 Do not forget to do charitable works, and to share with others, for God is well-pleased at such sacrifices. 17 Obey your leaders and be subject to them, for they are watching over your souls, since they will give an account for them, so that they may do so with joy and not with grief; for this would be no profit to you. 18 Pray for us, for we believe that we have a good conscience, and that we want to live a good life in all respects. 19 But much more, I beg you, pray that I might be restored to you sooner.

[16] 'Charitable works', **eupoiïâs**, literally, 'doing-good'.

'Share', **koinôniâs**, Vulg. *communionis*, i.e. 'sharing' material things. It has nothing to do with 'communion', i.e. the eucharist, in this context. Nor is there any hint that it has to do with sharing the gift of the Holy Spirit, or religious fellowship. **Koinôniâ** is clearly meant to be taken, like **eupoiïâ**, as the practical application of religious duty which pleases God. See note on 10.33.

[17] 'Leaders' is usually taken as referring to those with authority in the church, but can it be taken as a reference to civil authorities? The statement that they 'are watching over your souls (or lives)', **agrypnousin** (literally, 'they are staying awake') **hyper tôn psûchôn hûmôn**, seems a little over-stated, if it refers to the Roman officials they normally came into contact with. The fact, however, that our writer sees them as having to render an account to God does not mean that the verse cannot refer to secular authorities. All government, whether civil or religious, is responsible to God.

'Do so', can refer either to 'giving an account' or to 'watching over your souls'. On balance, the former is more likely.

[18] This verse need not be taken as suggesting that the writer feels that his message might meet with opposition, nor that he is assuring his audience that his conscience is clear on that subject. It is more likely that he is asking for their prayer to support him in his general work for the church, and is assuring them of his dedication to the cause, i.e. that he is a worthy object for their intercession. This is not pride or boasting on his part. Paul uses similar language in II Cor. 1.11–12, 'while you too are co-operating by interceding on our behalf, so that, for the gift bestowed on us through (the prayers of) many, many might give thanks for us. For our boast is the testimony of a good conscience, that our way of life in the world, and especially in regard to our dealings with you, has been one led by God's grace and God's simple sincerity, not worldly wisdom.' Note, incidentally, that our writer, like Paul, uses the author's plural 'we', even when he is obviously talking about himself.

[19] The writer reverts to the singular 'I', because this is, in a sense, a more personal request. He is anxious to see them soon, probably because of the concern expressed in his letter, that they were being tempted to return to Judaism.

'I might be restored', **apokatastathô**, could, as Montefiore points out, refer to recovery from illness or release from prison, but in the absence of evidence one way or the other, it is likely that he is simply expressing the wish to make the visit that he refers to in v. 23.

20 May the God of peace, who brought back from the dead our Lord Jesus, the great shepherd of the sheep, by the blood of the eternal covenant, 21 equip you with everything good for doing his will, working amongst us

what is well-pleasing before him, through Jesus Christ, to whom be glory for ever and ever, amen.

22 I beseech you, brothers and sisters, to put up with my message of admonishment, for indeed my letter to you is a brief one. 23 Know that our brother Timothy has left, and I shall see you with him, if he arrives soon. 24 Greet all your leaders and all the saints. Those from Italy greet you. 25 Grace be with you all.

[20–21] This prayer has the feel of a familiar liturgical passage. Is our writer simply quoting from an existing prayer, one which was composed by somebody else? Or did he compose it himself for this occasion?

[20] 'The God of peace' is an expression used by Paul in the closing prayer of his letter to the Romans. If this letter was also written to Roman Christians, it would be an interesting coincidence, and a reminder to them of the need to avoid dissension. As Montefiore remarks, it is particularly apt in this letter.

'The great shepherd of the sheep', **ton poimena tôn probatôn ton megan,** originates in Isa. 63.11, where the phrase 'shepherd of the sheep' is used to refer to Moses. Ezekiel 34.23 speaks of the Messiah as a shepherd, and Jesus describes himself as 'the good shepherd' in John 10.14. In I Peter 5.4 he is described as 'chief-shepherd', **archipoimên.**

[21] 'Amongst us', **en hêmîn,** seems an awkward transition from the 'you' of the earlier part of v. 21, but it is the better reading of the manuscripts. The AV translation was based on a different textual canon, and hence renders the pronoun as 'you'. It is very common to find textual confusion with 'we', **hêmeis,** and 'you', **hûmeis,** especially in the later period, when both words were pronounced the same way.

[22] This verse, and the succeeding ones, seem to us almost like a post-script, coming after the climax of the great prayer, but many of the NT letters have endings full of little messages which are rather like a succession of after-thoughts. What is remarkable about this one is the statement 'my letter to you is a brief one', **dia bracheôn epesteila hûmîn**. Since it is particularly long and it has been calculated that it would probably have taken nearly an hour to read aloud, I am driven to the conclusion that our writer must be joking. And why not? Every preacher has his little joke.

[23] 'Timothy' is the only name in this letter of any contemporary mentioned by our writer. He must be the famous companion of Paul, and was clearly known to the audience and to the writer of this letter. If our writer is Barnabas, this would not be surprising, as they had known each other since the early days when Paul and Barnabas worked closely together in the eastern Mediterranean area.

'Has left', **apolelymenon,** is an obscure reference, since the root meaning of this word is 'released'. This has led to the suggestion that Timothy had been in prison, but we have no evidence for that. The verb is often used to mean 'leave', but can also mean 'to be detached' or 'separated'. The likely scenario is that Timothy had left early to visit some other town, and that they were intending to meet up later and continue on their journey together.

[24] See the introduction for a discussion of the phrase 'those from Italy'. Montefiore suggests that they are Aquila and Prisca, who had come from Rome and settled in Ephesus, but, however plausible a hypothesis, we cannot prove it.

[25] 'Grace be with you all', is the same prayer as the one found at the end of the letter to Titus.

Bibliography

St John Chrysostom — *The Homilies on the Epistle to the Hebrews*, translated by T. Keble and revised by F. Gardiner, Vol. XIV of *A Select Library of the Nicene and Post-Nicene Fathers of the Christian Church*, edited by Philip Schaff. Published originally in 1889 and reprinted as Vol. XIV of *The Writings of the Nicene and Post-Nicene Fathers* (First Series), W. B. Eerdmans, Grand Rapids, Michigan 1956

H. T. Andrews — *Hebrews*, Abingdon Bible Commentary, Epworth Press, London 1929

W. Barclay — *The Letter to the Hebrews*, The Daily Study Bible series, The Saint Andrew Press, Edinburgh 1955

A. B. Bruce — *The Epistle to the Hebrews, The First Apology for Christianity*, T. & T. Clark, Edinburgh 1899

F. F. Bruce — 'Hebrews', *Peake's Commentary on the Bible*, Nelson, London 1962

S. C. Gayford — 'The Epistle to the Hebrews', *A New Commentary on Holy Scripture*, SPCK, London 1958

D. Guthrie

The Letter to the Hebrews: An Introduction and Commentary, Tyndale NT Commentaries, Inter-Varsity Press, Leicester 1983

J. Moffatt

A Critical and Exegetical Commentary on the Epistle to the Hebrews, T. & T. Clark, Edinburgh 1924

H. W. Montefiore

A Commentary on the Epistle to the Hebrews, Black's New Testament Commentaries, A. & C. Black, London 1964